REVISED EDITION

Dining In-Dallas

COOKBOOK

A Collection of Gourmet Recipes for Complete Meals from the Dallas Area's Finest Restaurants

MARILYN
WYRICK
INGRAM
and
LOIS
JOHNSON
FOLSE

Foreword by
WERNER VOGELI
President, Texas Chefs Association

PEANUT BUTTER
PUBLISHING

Peanut Butter Publishing
Mercer Island, Washington

TITLES IN SERIES

Feasting in Atlanta
Dining In–Baltimore
Dining In–Boston
Dining In–Chicago, Vol. I
Dining In–Chicago, Vol. II
Dining In–Cleveland
Dining In–Dallas, Revised
Dining In–Denver
Dining In–Hawaii
Dining In–Houston, Vol. I
Dining In–Houston, Vol. II
Dining In–Kansas City
Dining In–Los Angeles, Revised
Dining In–Milwaukee
Dining In–Minneapolis/St. Paul
Dining In–Minneapolis/St. Paul, Vol. II
Dining In–Monterey Peninsula
Feasting In New Orleans
Dining In–Philadelphia
Dining In–Phoenix
Dining In–Pittsburgh, Revised
Dining In–Portland
Dining In–St. Louis
Dining In–San Francisco
Dining In–Seattle, Vol. I
Dining In–Seattle, Vol. II
Dining In–Seattle, Vol. III
Dining In–Sun Valley
Dining In–Washington, D.C.

Dining In–Toronto
Dining In–Vancouver, B.C.

Cover photograph by Jean François Stien
Cover design and illustrations by Neil Sweeney

CONTENTS

FOREWORD

Dallas has a reputation of striving to be the best in many ways. Certainly this holds true for its distinctive dining tradition. Dallas's large number of outstanding restaurants offers a variety of cuisines which is as good or better than that available in most cities in the world. One can choose from Continental, Oriental, Italian, Tex-Mex, and good "down home" cooking, to name a few. Dallas's restaurants are operated by experienced and talented owners and chefs. Many of my chef friends are transplanted here from France, Germany, Switzerland, Italy, Spain, and Austria, and others are from the Far East, the Pacific, and Mexico, each bringing with him knowledge of the unique cuisine from his native land.

This newly revised edition of *Dining In–Dallas* includes menus and recipes from some of the best of our celebrated restaurants. It was no simple task to select the restaurants, and even more difficult singling out the best of their courses. Although we do not endorse any restaurant, we do vouch for the excellent quality of the recipes.

Since cooking is my profession and dining my pleasure, I am certain you, too, will find *Dining In–Dallas* a joy whether you dine in or out. Bon Appetit!

Werner Vogeli
President, Texas Chefs Asociation

Dinner for Four

Mushroom Soup à L'Ambiance

Bay Scallops in Ginger Sauce

Asparagus Vinaigrette

Salmon with Mustard Sauce

Carrot Terrine

Fresh Spinach with Romano Cheese

Turnip Mousse

Dauphinoise Potatoes Gratin

Concorde Cake

Beverages:
With the Scallops—Beaulieu Vineyards Sauvignon Blanc
With the Salmon—Pouilly-Fumé, La Doucette
With the Cake—crème de menthe

Morris & Esther Robbins, Owners
John L. Weber, Chef

L'AMBIANCE

*M*orris Robbins had been a meat purveyor for twenty-eight years when he and his wife Esther decided to jointly venture into the creative end of the the food industry. They selected the site, a converted Shell service station, and L'Ambiance soon established a reputation in the Dallas area as a charming and intimate French restaurant.

Chef John L. Weber has been at L'Ambiance since its inception, first as sous-chef and now as executive chef. Under his direction, the menu offers nouvelle cuisine at its best—imaginative, delicate, and perfectly prepared. Using fresh ingredients as often as possible, especially vegetables, insures the excellence of the dishes.

Dallasites and tourists alike can always be found crowded into L'Ambiance, and as a result, are always sure to be enjoying themselves.

2408 Cedar Springs

MUSHROOM SOUP A L'AMBIANCE

¼ cup clarified butter
1 tablespoon finely chopped
  shallots
¾ pound fresh mushrooms,
  finely chopped
2 tablespoons port wine

2 cups milk
2 cups whipping cream
1 tablespoon butter, softened
1 tablespoon all-purpose flour
  Salt and pepper to taste

1. Melt the clarified butter in a medium saucepan over high heat; sauté the shallots for 2 minutes. Add the mushrooms and sauté until most of the liquid is gone.
2. Stir in the port and cook until well absorbed.
3. Add the milk and cream. Bring to a boil and reduce heat to a simmer; cook 10 minutes.
4. Form a beurre manié by kneading together the softened butter and flour into a walnut-size ball.
5. Season the soup with salt and pepper. Thicken by incorporating the beurre manié in small bits. Serve hot.

Note: To clarify butter, place in a small saucepan and melt it over low heat. Eventually a foamy residue will form on top. Spoon off the foam and pour the clarified butter into a container, leaving any bottom residue in the pan to discard.

Use a touch more port if a slightly sweeter flavor is desired.

BAY SCALLOPS IN GINGER SAUCE

¾ cup whipping cream
¼ cup dry white wine
1 tablespoon finely chopped shallots
1 teaspoon grated fresh gingerroot

1 pound fresh bay scallops
2 tablespoons unsalted butter
Salt
White pepper
¼ cup stiffly whipped cream

1. Place the whipping cream, wine, shallots, and grated ginger in a saucepan and bring to a boil. Add the scallops and cook quickly for 2 to 3 minutes. The resulting mixture should leave the scallops coated with a creamy glaze. Remove from heat.
2. Gently whisk in bits of the unsalted butter. Add salt and white pepper to taste. Fold in the whipped cream.
3. Divide the mixture into four coquille shells and place under a hot broiler just prior to serving, so that the sauce is bubbly and beautifully browned. Be careful not to scorch.

The longer scallops cook, the tougher they become. The secret is to balance the amount of cream and wine so the sauce thickens to a glaze just as the scallops become done.

Sea scallops may be used if bay scallops are not available, but they are a little less tender and not so delicately flavored.

ASPARAGUS VINAIGRETTE

1½ pounds fresh jumbo
    California asparagus
4 leaves Boston lettuce

4 slices tomato
   SAUCE VINAIGRETTE

1. Cut off the tough stems of the asparagus so that each spear is approximately 6 inches long. Peel the lower half of each spear.
2. Boil covered in lightly salted water until crisp-tender. Immediately drain and chill slightly; if the asparagus becomes too cold, it will be less flavorful.
3. On each of four chilled salad plates, place one lettuce leaf topped with one tomato slice. Arrange several asparagus spears side by side on top. Cover with the sauce, leaving the green tips of the spears exposed.

SAUCE VINAIGRETTE

1 egg yolk
⅓ cup Dijon mustard
2 teaspoons tarragon vinegar
1 tablespoon Temeraire
   mustard
¼ cup red wine vinegar

2½ cups soybean or salad oil
   Salt
   White pepper
2 tablespoons red burgundy
   wine

1. Using an electric mixer, beat the egg yolk briefly at low speed. Add the Dijon mustard, tarragon vinegar, Temeraire mustard, and red wine vinegar while continuing to beat.
2. Still beating at low speed, drizzle in the oil until the mixture thickens slightly to the consistency of a thin mayonnaise.
3. Season with salt and white pepper; incorporate the wine. Chill before serving.

Temeraire mustard is available in specialty food stores.

We use this same sauce with our luncheon chicken and seafood salads. Delicious!

SALMON WITH MUSTARD SAUCE

4 (6-ounce) fresh king
  salmon fillets
1½ cups whipping cream
⅓ cup dry white wine
2 tablespoons finely chopped
  shallots

¼ teaspoon thyme
Salt
White pepper
MUSTARD SAUCE

1. Preheat oven to 450°.
2. Arrange the salmon fillets in a single layer in a baking dish. Combine the cream, wine, shallots, thyme, salt, and white pepper and pour over the fish. Bake uncovered in preheated oven until springy to the touch and slightly undercooked.
3. Strain the cooking liquid and reserve for the sauce. Place one fillet on each of four serving plates and keep warm in a low oven set at 150° while preparing the sauce.
4. At serving time, baste each fish with a generous portion of the sauce and place under a hot broiler to glaze until beautifully browned, being careful not to scorch.

At L'Ambiance we also arrange four vegetable servings on the same plate before glazing under the broiler. The plates of food are immediately presented to our diners while still very hot.

MUSTARD SAUCE

Reserved cooking liquid
3 tablespoons unsalted
  butter

2 teaspoons Dijon mustard
  (approximately)
½ cup stiffly whipped cream

Heat the cooking liquid in a saucepan over medium heat; cook until bubbly and thick. Remove from heat and whisk in the butter until melted. Return to heat, but do not let boil. Incorporate the mustard and whipped cream until well blended.

CARROT TERRINE

2 pounds carrots, peeled
   and very thinly sliced
4 tablespoons unsalted butter
   Salt
   White pepper

5 whole eggs
2 egg yolks
2 tablespoons orange flower
   water (approximately)

1. Place the carrots in a saucepan; add enough water to barely cover and add the butter, salt, and white pepper. Stirring frequently, steam over medium heat until tender enough to cut with a fork; do not overcook. Drain, reserving the liquid, and set the carrots aside.
2. Preheat oven to 450°.
3. Return the liquid to the saucepan and cook until reduced to ½ cup. Cool.
4. Beat together the whole eggs, egg yolks, and orange flower water to taste. Add the carrot liquid and stir to incorporate. Fold in the carrots.
5. Line a 9-inch by 5-inch by 3-inch glass loaf pan with buttered waxed paper. Spoon the carrot mixture into the pan and cover with foil. Set the loaf pan in a larger pan and add boiling water to the larger pan to a depth of 1 to 2 inches to make a bain-marie. Bake in preheated oven until a knife inserted comes out clean, about 1 hour and 15 minutes. Chill the loaf 30 minutes.
6. Loosen the edges of the loaf with a spatula, invert onto a plate, and remove the waxed paper. Slice the loaf in half lengthwise, then crosswise into individual servings. Place on a serving plate and re-heat at 200° until heated through.

Note: A glass pan is preferable for baking the loaf as metal may discolor the carrots. Depending on the size of the slices, this recipe should serve twelve.

Orange flower water is available at specialty food stores.

FRESH SPINACH WITH ROMANO CHEESE

2 *pounds fresh spinach,*
  washed, stems removed
4 *tablespoons unsalted butter*

Salt and pepper to taste
½ *cup grated fresh Romano*
  cheese

1. Boil the spinach in lightly salted water for 3 minutes or until tender. Drain in a colander, submerge in cold water to shock, and squeeze until partially dry. Chop coarsely.
2. Melt the butter in a saucepan; add salt and pepper. Add the spinach and stir until heated.
3. Add the cheese and continue to heat and stir until the cheese melts and is absorbed. Serve hot.

TURNIP MOUSSE

¾ *pound turnips, peeled and*
  coarsely chopped
1 *large potato, peeled and*
  coarsely chopped
3 *tablespoons unsalted butter*

⅓ *cup whipping cream*
  (approximately)
Salt
White pepper

1. Boil together the turnips and potatoes in lightly salted water until tender. Drain in a colander and press the vegetables with a small bowl to squeeze dry.
2. Purée the dry vegetable mixture. Whip in the butter and add enough cream to moisten. Season with salt and white pepper. Place in a casserole dish and set the dish in a pan of hot water. Keep warm in a low oven until serving time.

Note: If the turnips have a sharp taste, add a pinch of sugar.

This recipe is of the old Southern tradition rather than French. It is so popular that some of our clientele insist on it each time they dine with us.

DAUPHINOISE POTATOES GRATIN

1½ pounds high-quality red potatoes	Salt
¾ cup milk	White pepper
¾ cup whipping cream	½ cup grated Jarlsberg cheese
1 clove garlic, finely chopped	Additional cream, for glazing

1. Preheat oven to 450°.
2. Peel and slice the potatoes ⅛ inch thick. Place in a 1½-quart buttered casserole. Combine the milk, cream, garlic, salt, and white pepper and pour over the potatoes.
3. Set the casserole dish in a larger pan and add boiling water to the larger pan to a depth of 1 to 2 inches to make a bain-marie. Bake uncovered in preheated oven 1½ hours, adding water as needed to the larger pan.
4. Remove the potatoes and spread on a large flat tray. Sprinkle with the grated cheese and drizzle additional cream over the surface. Glaze under a hot broiler until browned and bubbly.

Note: Grated Gruyère or a good Swiss cheese may be used, but Jarlsberg gives the finest flavor.

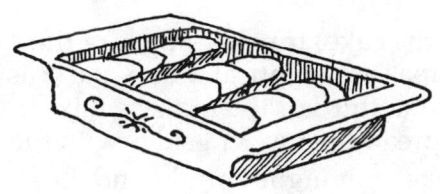

CONCORDE CAKE

1¼ cups egg whites
     (approximately 10 large
     eggs)
 1 cup granulated sugar
1½ cups powdered sugar
1½ teaspoons powdered cocoa

*CHOCOLATE MOUSSE
FILLING*
 2 ounces sliced almonds,
     toasted
*Powdered sugar, for
dusting*

1. Line a large sheet pan with parchment paper. Using a round 8-inch cake pan as the guide, trace the outline of two circles on the parchment paper. Set aside.
2. Preheat oven to 275°.
3. Beat the egg whites with an electric mixer until soft peaks form. Add one-half of the granulated sugar and continue beating. When stiff, add the remaining granulated sugar and beat until very stiff but not dry.
4. Sift together the powdered sugar and cocoa and quickly fold into the egg white mixture using a rubber spatula. Fit a pastry bag with a large round tube; fill the bag with this meringue mixture and pipe concentric circles onto the circles on the parchment paper so that each circle is completely covered. With the remaining meringue, pipe long, straight strips alongside the circles.
5. Bake in preheated oven 1 hour and 15 minutes. Be sure not to overcook, or the crusts will become too brittle and break apart. Remove from oven to cool and crisp. When cool, break the long strips into chunks.
6. To assemble the cake, trim the edges of the two meringue crusts so that their shapes are identical. Place one crust on a cake platter and spread with one-third of the mousse mixture. Place the other crust on top and spread the top and sides with the remaining mousse.
7. Press the broken meringue chunks and the almonds into the top and sides of the mousse-covered cake. Dust the surface with powdered sugar. Chill until set. Cut into twelve wedges. Remove from refrigerator 30 minutes before serving for a creamier mousse.

Note: For a decorative pattern, lay 1-inch strips of foil in a criss-cross pattern on top of the cake before dusting with powdered sugar. Remove the foil after the sugar has been added.

Use the meringue right away, especially on damp or humid days.

At L'Ambiance we make two of these cakes every afternoon at five o'clock. By closing time there is not a piece remaining.

CHOCOLATE MOUSSE FILLING

5½ ounces semisweet German chocolate (preferably Carma brand)	¾ cup egg whites (approximately 6 large eggs)
7 tablespoons unsalted butter	¼ cup sugar
3 egg yolks	

1. Place the chocolate and butter in the top portion of a double boiler and melt over simmering water. Whisk in the egg yolks one at a time until each is incorporated into the chocolate mixture. Chill 10 minutes or until the mixture thickens to the consistency of a heavy cream.
2. Using an electric mixer, beat the egg whites until soft peaks form. Gradually beat in the sugar; continue beating until stiff but not dry. Carefully fold the stiffly beaten egg whites into the chocolate mixture. Chill 20 minutes before spreading on the meringue crusts.

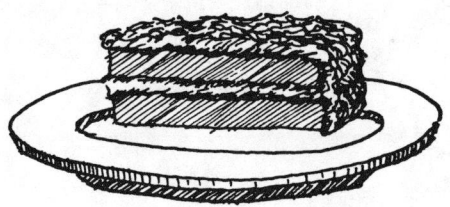

Bagatelle

Dinner for Six

Chicken Almond Soup

Shrimp du Chef
with
Brown Burgundy Sauce

Hearts of Palm Salad
with
Lime Dressing

Roast Duck à la Normande

Rice Pilaf

Broccoli Noisette

Chocolate Mousse Amaretto

Wine:
With the Soup—Dry Sack Sherry
With the Shrimp—Marquis de Goulaine Muscadet
With the Duck—Gevrey-Chambertin
With the Mousse—Gancia Asti Spumante

Leodegar Meier, President

*T*he Bagatelle may be located in a modern office building, but its view of trees and a fountain on a quiet plaza takes one away from the bustle of business and into a comfortable French country setting that maintains a happy balance between the formal and informal.

Owner Leodegar Meier brings to Dallas a colorful background which explains the originality of his culinary expertise. Born and educated in Switzerland, he was trained first as a chef, later additionally studying other aspects of hotel and restaurant service including management. A born traveler, he says he got into the restaurant business "to have a trade I could travel with." The profession certainly has served him well, considering that England, Panama, Chicago, and Pittsburgh preceded his move to Dallas.

"Our cuisine is classic French," Leodegar states, "but with some variations since we have developed some of our own recipes as well." Good food, hospitably served and reasonably priced, is the basis of the philsolphy by which he runs the Bagatelle and is, no doubt, one of the major reasons for its success.

One Energy Plaza
4925 Greenville Avenue

CHICKEN ALMOND SOUP

¼ pound butter
2 tablespoons flour
1 quart Chicken Stock
  (see index)
6 ounces blanched almonds,
  sliced
  Salt and white pepper
  to taste

2 ounces dry sherry
⅓ cup finely diced cooked
  chicken meat
1 pint heavy cream
2 egg yolks

1. Preheat oven to 300°.
2. Stir the butter and flour together in a saucepan over medium heat. Cook 4 minutes, stirring constantly. Stir in the chicken stock and bring to a boil. Reduce heat and keep warm.
3. Place the almonds on a cookie sheet and toast to a golden color in preheated oven, turning frequently. Remove. Reserve one-half and finely chop the remainder.
4. Mix the chopped almonds into the soup. Add the salt, white pepper, sherry, and chicken meat.
5. Mix the cream and egg yolks together. Remove soup from heat and lace the cream/egg mixture in, stirring constantly with a wooden spoon. Ladle into six bowls and garnish with the reserved toasted almond slices.

SHRIMP DU CHEF

Oil for deep-frying
18 *shrimp, peeled, deveined,*
and butterflied
½ *cup rice flour*
¼ *pound butter*
2 *cloves garlic, finely*
chopped

¼ *cup parsley, chopped*
1 *lemon*
BROWN BURGUNDY
SAUCE
Lemon slices
Parsley sprigs

1. Heat the oil to 350° in a deep-fryer or deep pan.
2. Coat the shrimp with rice flour. Deep-fry for 10 seconds; drain.
3. Heat the butter in a skillet; add the garlic and chopped parsley.
4. Add the shrimp and sauté 3 to 4 minutes.
5. Squeeze the lemon juice over shrimp. Serve the shrimp in coquille shells with Brown Burgundy Sauce, garnished with lemon slices and parsley.

BROWN BURGUNDY SAUCE

1 *tablespoon butter*
1 *tablespoon all-purpose*
flour

½ *cup beef bouillon*
Salt and pepper
2 *tablespoons burgundy*

1. Melt the butter in a saucepan; stir in the flour until blended.
2. Slowly add the bouillon, stirring constantly. Cook and stir until the mixture reaches a boil.
3. Stir in salt and pepper to taste and the burgundy.

HEARTS OF PALM SALAD

6 heads limestone lettuce	6 radish roses
12 ounces canned hearts of palm	1 bunch parsley, well washed
6 plum tomatoes	LIME DRESSING

1. Pull lettuce leaves apart and wash in cold water; shake off water thoroughly.
2. Arrange lettuce neatly on individual plates.
3. Slice the hearts of palm into ¼-inch discs; arrange on top of lettuce.
4. Cut the tomatoes in half. Arrange with the radish roses and parsley in a neat garnish. Drizzle with Lime Dressing and serve.

If limestone lettuce is not available, substitute Boston lettuce.

LIME DRESSING

1 cup salad oil	1 teaspoon sugar
Juice of 3 limes	1 tablespoon chopped parsley
Salt and white pepper to taste	

Whip the oil with the lime juice. Add the remaining ingredients and mix well.

ROAST DUCK A LA NORMANDE

2 (5 to 6-pound) ducks,
  dressed for roasting
1 teaspoon salt
1 teaspoon pepper
1 teaspoon thyme
5 large apples

Juice of 1 lemon
¾ cup cranberry sauce
3 ounces Calvados (apple
  brandy)
CIDER CREAM SAUCE

1. Preheat oven to 400°.
2. Season the insides of the ducks with salt, pepper, and thyme.
3. Cut 2 apples in coarse pieces and stuff into the ducks. Place the ducks breast down in deep roasting pans. Add a quart of hot water to each and cook in preheated oven until the water has evaporated, about 45 minutes.
4. Turn the ducks breast up; pour off excess fat. Continue roasting, basting regularly until well done, approximately 1½ hours.
5. While the ducks are roasting, cut three apples in half. Core and poach in water with the lemon juice until tender.
6. Place 2 tablespoons cranberry sauce in each apple and place in the oven with the ducks to warm.
7. When ducks are done, remove from oven and set aside briefly until cooled enough to handle. Bone the ducks and cut into six portions. Reserve the bones and drippings.
8. Pour the Calvados over the ducks and flame.
9. Pour Cider Cream Sauce over, surround with stuffed apples, and serve.

CIDER CREAM SAUCE

Duck bones and drippings
2 medium-size onions, sliced
3 tablespoons all-purpose
flour
2 tablespoons currant jelly

1 pint apple cider
Salt and pepper to taste
1 cup heavy cream
¼ cup Calvados (apple
brandy)

1. Pour off the fat from the duck roasting pan, reserving about 2 tablespoons. Scrape the drippings into a container and reserve.
2. Return the reserved duck fat to the pan. Heat and add the onions and flour, sautéing until browned.
3. Add the currant jelly, duck bones, reserved drippings, apple cider, and salt and pepper. Simmer 30 minutes.
4. Strain the mixture into a saucepan. Add the cream and simmer 10 minutes. Stir in the Calvados and remove from heat.

RICE PILAF

4 tablespoons butter
2 tablespoons finely
chopped onion
1 cup long-grain rice
1 cup Chicken Stock (see
index) or 2 chicken
bouillon cubes dissolved
in 1 cup water

Salt
White pepper

1. Melt the butter in a saucepan. Add the onion and sauté until light brown.
2. Add the rice and toast 2 minutes, stirring constantly, over medium heat.
3. Add the chicken stock and simmer, covered, until the liquid is absorbed, stirring occasionally (about 20 minutes).
4. Add salt and white pepper to taste.

BROCCOLI NOISETTE

1 tablespoon salt
2 pounds fresh broccoli,
   trimmed
¼ cup bread crumbs

1 ounce Parmesan cheese,
   grated
¼ pound butter

1. Bring 1 quart water and the salt to a boil in a shallow saucepan.
2. Place the broccoli in the pan and simmer until crisp-tender. Drain the broccoli and place on a serving platter.
3. Sprinkle with the bread crumbs and grated cheese.
4. Brown the butter in a skillet. Pour over the broccoli and serve.

CHOCOLATE MOUSSE AMARETTO

8 ounces semisweet
   chocolate
5 egg yolks
1 pint whipping cream
5 ounces sliced, blanched
   almonds, toasted

1 teaspoon vanilla extract
¼ cup chocolate syrup
3 ounces amaretto
   Pinch of salt
1 ounce chocolate, shaved

1. Melt the semisweet chocolate over low heat.
2. Whip the egg yolks and 3 tablespoons water in a double boiler until frothy; immediately cool the bowl in ice.
3. Whip the cream to soft peaks. Reserve a small amount for topping.
4. Combine the chocolate, egg yolks, whipped cream, almonds, vanilla extract, chocolate syrup, amaretto, and salt. Spoon into dessert dishes and freeze 2 hours.
5. Transfer the mousse to refrigerator for 15 to 20 minutes until thawed but still very cold.
6. Top each serving with whipped cream and chocolate shavings and serve.

Freezing the mousse allows the dessert to be held for several days without fear of the eggs spoiling.

 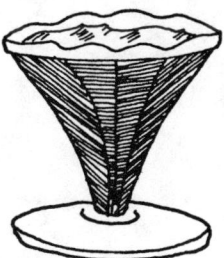

BUGATTI

Dinner for Four

Crab Claws Stefano

Fresh Mushroom Soup

Bugatti's Italian Salad

Veal Fiorentina

Zucchini with Onions and Mushrooms

Oven-Roast Potatoes

Bigné alla Romana

Wine:
With the Crab—Verdicchio
With the Veal—Barolo, Antinori

Mario Perez & Stefano Carrelli, Owners
Stefano Carrelli, Chef

*B*ugatti restaurant attracts and welcomes a diverse clientele, with lawyers and laborers seated side by side. This is due, no doubt, to the fact that its outstanding Italian cuisine is universally loved by all.

Co-Owner and Chef Stefano Carrelli, whose professional apprenticeship began at age fifteen, has worked in countless major European cities as well as on the cruise ship Poseidon. He met Co-Owner Mario Perez, a native of Madrid, while both were employed at another Dallas restaurant. They run their restaurant with a European philosophy of cuisine and kitchen management, and they never lose sight of their primary goal—to make their friends happy with fabulous food.

2574 Walnut Hill Lane

CRAB CLAWS STEFANO

4 tablespoons butter
1 clove garlic, chopped
½ cup dry white wine
1 tablespoon chopped parsley

½ teaspoon instant chicken
   bouillon granules
Salt and pepper to taste
16 crab claws

1. Melt the butter in a sauté pan over medium-high heat. Add the garlic and sauté briefly.
2. Add the white wine, parsley, chicken bouillon, and salt and pepper. Stir. Add the crab claws and sauté for 2 minutes. Serve hot, four claws per serving.

FRESH MUSHROOM SOUP

12 medium-size mushrooms, chopped
⅓ cup chopped onion
4 tablespoons butter
3 cups WHITE CREAM SAUCE

1 teaspoon instant chicken bouillon granules
Salt and pepper to taste
1 cup whipping cream

1. Sauté the mushrooms and onion in the butter until the onion is transparent. Do not brown.
2. Add the White Cream Sauce and simmer for 20 minutes.
3. Season with chicken bouillon and salt and pepper to taste.
4. Stir the cream into the soup. Continue to cook until it begins to boil. Remove immediately and serve while hot.

WHITE CREAM SAUCE

4 tablespoons butter
¼ cup flour

3 cups milk
Dash of nutmeg

1. Melt the butter in a small saucepan. Stir in the flour to form a roux. Simmer over low heat about 5 minutes, or until the flour is cooked but not browned, stirring constantly.
2. Add the milk all at once. Increase heat and stir continuously until smooth and thickened. Season to taste with nutmeg.

BUGATTI'S ITALIAN SALAD

1 *head romaine lettuce, torn*
  into bite-size pieces
2 *tomatoes, cut in wedges*
2 *tablespoons chopped onion*
2 *tablespoons chopped parsley*

8 *black olives, sliced*
8 *green olives, sliced*
  ITALIAN DRESSING
  Grated Romano cheese

1. Arrange the lettuce and tomatoes on each of four salad plates.
2. Arrange the onion, parsley, and both kinds of olives attractively over the lettuce.
3. Top with Italian Dressing and a generous sprinking of grated Romano cheese.

ITALIAN DRESSING

¾ *cup olive oil*
¼ *cup red wine vinegar*
1 *teaspoon dry mustard*

1 *tablespoon finely chopped*
  onion
  Salt and pepper to taste

Blend all ingredients together.

VEAL FIORENTINA

4 (6-ounce) veal scallops
Flour
¼ pound butter
½ pound fresh spinach,
    chopped and steamed

½ pound fresh lump crabmeat
HOLLANDAISE SAUCE

1. Preheat oven to 350°.
2. Slice each scallop in half, making eight thin scallops. Pound each slice to flatten.
3. Dust scallops with flour and sauté in butter, turning once, until lightly browned on both sides.
4. Divide the cooked spinach into four portions and place on a baking sheet. Cover each portion with two scallops.
5. Divide the crab into four portions and arrange attractively on top of the scallops.
6. Top with an ample portion of Hollandaise Sauce and place in preheated oven just until the scallops are heated. Do not brown the sauce. Remove each portion to a plate and serve at once.

HOLLANDAISE SAUCE

¾ pound butter
3 tablespoons boiling water
2 tablespoons lemon juice
4 egg yolks
2 dashes of Tabasco sauce

1 teaspoon Worcestershire
  sauce
Salt
White pepper

1. Melt the butter slowly in a saucepan. Skim the foam. Pour off the clear butterfat, retaining the milky solids in the pan. Discard the solids; keep the clarified butter warm.
2. Heat the water and lemon juice.
3. Place the egg yolks in a blender container and blend at low speed for 1 minute.
4. Add the water and lemon juice while continuing to blend at low speed.
5. Add the butter and remaining seasonings and turn to high speed briefly until thick and creamy.

ZUCCHINI WITH ONIONS AND MUSHROOMS

4 *medium-size zucchini,*
      unpeeled
4 *tablespoons butter*
6 *mushrooms, sliced*

¼ *cup chopped onion*
½ *teaspoon chopped garlic*
    Salt and pepper to taste

1. Chop the zucchini coarsely. Boil covered in water until zucchini is al dente (crisp-tender). Drain.
2. Melt the butter in a skillet and sauté the mushrooms and onion until the onion is clear. Do not brown.
3. Add the zucchini, garlic, and salt and pepper and sauté for 2 minutes. Serve immediately while very hot.

OVEN-ROAST POTATOES

2 *large baking potatoes,*
      peeled and coarsely
      chopped

½ *cup white wine*
3 *tablespoons butter, melted*
    Salt and pepper

Preheat oven to 350°. Mix the chopped potatoes with the wine, butter, salt, and pepper. Place in a covered casserole and bake for 35 to 40 minutes or until done. Moisten with water during the baking, if necessary.

BIGNÉ ALLA ROMANA

4 tablespoons butter, cut
    into small pieces
¼ teaspoon salt
1 tablespoon sugar
1 cup sifted all-purpose flour

4 eggs
CRÈME PARISIENNE
Chocolate syrup
WHIPPED CREAM

1. Preheat oven to 375°.
2. Place 1 cup water, the butter, salt, and sugar in a heavy saucepan. Bring the mixture to a boil to melt the butter and dissolve the sugar. Remove from heat.
3. Add the flour all at once and stir vigorously. Return the pan to medium heat for 2 minutes, or until the dough forms a ball when stirred. Remove from heat.
4. Add the eggs one at a time, beating well after each addition.
5. Butter and flour a baking sheet. Using two spoons or a pastry bag, form egg-size balls of dough and place 3 inches apart on the sheet.
6. Bake in preheated oven for 25 minutes or until puffed and golden. Allow to cool.
7. Slice the tops off the cream puffs. Fill with Crème Parisienne. Chill.
8. Serve with chocolate syrup and Whipped Cream for topping.

CRÈME PARISIENNE

1 cup milk	5 egg yolks
1 cup whipping cream	¾ cup flour
1 cup sugar	1 teaspoon vanilla extract

1. Combine the milk and cream in a heavy saucepan. Carefully bring to a simmer.
2. Beat together the sugar and egg yolks until thick and lemon colored. Beat in the flour until smooth.
3. Stir in the simmering milk and cream. Place in a saucepan over moderate heat. Stir continuously while cooking to form a medium-thick custard.
4. Stir in the vanilla extract. Allow to cool before using.

WHIPPED CREAM

½ cup whipping cream	½ teaspoon vanilla extract
2 tablespoons sugar	

Whip the cream on high speed of an electric mixer, gradually adding the sugar and vanilla as it thickens. Continue beating until very stiff. Chill.

Chiquita

MEXICAN CUISINE

Dinner for Four

Sopa de Tortillas

Guacamole Salad

Chiles Rellenos

Sopaipillas

Wine:

Pedro Domecq Los Reyes Blanco

Mario Leal, Owner

Tino Trujillo, Chef

*E*ver since Mario Leal emigrated to Texas from Mexico, he has dreamed of showing people that Mexican food is much, much more than enchiladas. "People too often have a certain image of Mexican food—that it's spicy and greasy," says Mario. "If it is, it's a lousy cook making it that way. My food is not hot, but we do keep hot sauce on the tables for anyone who wants it."

Although one can order tacos or enchiladas at Chiquita, Mario strongly encourages his diners to try one of his beef, pork, chicken, or fish dishes, all of which are prepared in the truest Mexican tradition. Many meats are marinated, and all have received some extra care before being cooked. Side dishes are carefully selected to complement the entrée because, for example, "beans are good, but to serve beans with fish would kill the taste of the fish."

Mario has always believed that Dallasites are "more sophisticated than a bowl of chili." It has taken time and patience to educate his patrons, but he is rewarded now by customers who are so regular that they have the menu memorized.

3810 Congress Avenue

SOPA DE TORTILLAS

3 corn tortillas	1 hard-cooked egg, chopped
2½ cups corn oil	½ teaspoon ground cumin
1 clove garlic	¼ teaspoon black pepper
1 tomato	1 cup grated Monterey Jack
½ onion	cheese
6 cups Chicken Stock (see index)	1 avocado, sliced (optional)

1. Cut the tortillas into narrow pie-shaped wedges. Fry in hot oil until crisp. Drain on paper towels.
2. Pour off all but 1 tablespoon of the oil. Set the pan aside.
3. Purée the garlic, tomato, and onion in a blender. Sauté the purée in the pan with the remaining tablespoon of oil, stirring constantly, for 3 minutes.
4. Add the chicken stock, chopped egg, cumin, and pepper and simmer for 15 minutes.
5. Divide the fried tortilla strips in four soup bowls. Sprinkle ¼ cup cheese over each. Ladle the soup over. Garnish with sliced avocado if desired.

You can use the same oil by frying the Sopaipillas first, then the tortilla strips, and then the Chiles Rellenos.

GUACAMOLE SALAD

2 *avocados*
¼ *small onion*
½ *fresh tomato*
½ *lime*

1 *teaspoon salt*
Pinch of garlic salt
4 *lettuce leaves*

1. Peel and mash the avocados.
2. Chop the onion and tomato finely.
3. Squeeze the juice from the lime half over the mashed avocado. Mix with the chopped onion and tomato. Season with the salt and garlic to taste.
4. Serve on lettuce leaves with the Chiles Rellenos.

Guacamole will turn dark after a time, so if it is made more than an hour ahead, retain its bright color by submerging an avocado pit in it.

The word guacamole *comes from the Nahuatl words* ahuacatl *(avocado) and* molli *(a mixture).*

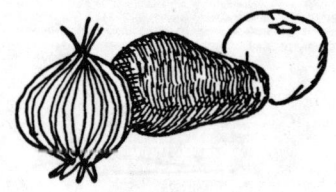

CHILES RELLENOS

6 *fresh chiles poblanos*
1 *pound ground sirloin*
½ *cup chopped onion*
2 *cloves garlic, chopped*
1 *teaspoon cumin*
1 *teaspoon black pepper*

1 *tablespoon salt*
Flour
Corn oil for deep-frying
6 *eggs, separated*
SALSA RANCHERA (see next page)

1. Preheat oven to 350°. Select the four chiles that are closest in size. Bake until the skins puff, about 25 minutes. Remove from oven and cover with a wet cloth or towel for 5 minutes.
2. Peel the skins off. Make a slit in each chile and remove all seeds, being gentle to avoid tearing the chiles.
3. Put 1 cup water and the meat in a saucepan and bring to a simmer. Cook at the simmering point until most of the liquid has evaporated. If any grease comes to the top, it should be skimmed off.
4. Cut the remaining chiles into narrow strips. Add these with the onion, garlic, cumin, pepper, and salt to the meat mixture when it appears to be starting to get dry. Cook a few minutes longer.
5. Stuff the chiles with meat mixture, then dust with flour. Begin heating the oil slowly.
6. Beat the egg whites until they peak. Beat the yolks until creamy. Fold the yolks into the whites.
7. Dip the chiles one at a time into the eggs. Gently place two chiles at a time into the hot oil. With a spatula, bathe the chiles with hot oil until the egg appears to have set. Cook 4 minutes, then turn and cook another 4 minutes. Drain on paper towels and keep warm. Repeat the process with the remaining chiles.
8. To serve, spoon a little Salsa Ranchera over the chiles and serve the remaining sauce in a bowl.

Chiles poblanos are the large, green, fairly mild chiles that are the usual variety in commercial canned chiles.

SALSA RANCHERA

½ onion
½ bell pepper
1 clove garlic
3 chiles, serrano or jalapeño

3 tomatoes
1 tablespoon oil
1 teaspoon salt

1. Chop all the vegetables.
2. Sauté the onion, bell pepper, and garlic in oil until soft, but do not brown.
3. Place in a blender with the chiles, tomatoes, salt, and 2 cups hot water. Purée.
4. Pour into a saucepan and simmer slowly for 10 minutes. Be careful not to dry it out.

The blender is probably the biggest boon to Mexican food preparation. Until its invention, one had to use a molcajete—*a mortar made of volcanic rock—and* tejolote, *or pestle, made from a grayish-black stone. These culinary implements were used for 3,500 years in Mexico.*

SOPAIPILLAS

4 cups sifted flour
1 tablespoon baking powder
1½ teaspoons salt
3 tablespoons granulated
  sugar
1 tablespoon shortening

1 cake compressed yeast
¼ cup warm water
1¼ cups scalded milk, cooled
  to room temperature
2 tablespoons cinnamon
  Honey (optional)

1. Combine the flour, baking powder, salt, and 1 tablespoon sugar. Cut in the shortening.
2. Dissolve the yeast in lukewarm water and add to the scalded milk.
3. Make a well in the center of the dry ingredients. Add the liquid and work into the dough. Knead the dough 15 to 20 times. Set aside about 10 minutes.
4. Roll the dough to ¼-inch thickness. Cut into triangles.
5. Fry in very hot corn oil (420°, if you have a fat thermometer), a few at a time, until puffy and golden. Drain.
6. Combine the remaining sugar with the cinnamon. Dust the sopaipillas with the mixture. Drizzle with honey, if desired, before serving.

Note: Fry only a few sopaipillas at a time so the fat will stay hot. They should puff up and become hollow immediately.

Dinner for Eight

Zucchini Coins

Cream of Mushroom Soup

Cheese Crackers

Dinner Salad, Crackers Style
with
Blue Cheese Dressing

Beef Burgundy
with
Reames Noodles

Broiler Tomatoes

Bread Pudding with Brandy Sauce

Royal Street Coffee

Wine:
Valpolicella, Bolla
or
Sebastiani Cabernet Sauvignon
or
Beaujolais, Sichel

Gus Katsigris, Owner

*S*haded by magnolia trees, tucked between antique stores and specialty shops on a small Dallas side street, Crackers is housed in a beautifully restored turn-of-the-century family mansion. Inside, a casual atmosphere is created by large, airy windows, green plants, lively graphics, and scattered café tables . . . even a second story balcony where guests enjoy alfresco dining.

As eclectic as the furnishings, Crackers' menu starts with a delightful cream-based soup complemented by tangy cheddar crackers. Next a crisp green dinner salad served with crunchy sesame breadsticks. Then a choice of entrées ranging from filet of sole to beef Burgundy to moussaka, the spicy house specialty.

Patrons are welcomed by Owner Gus Katsigris, a warm and jovial Greek who strolls through the restaurant greeting regular customers, inquiring about the food, and encouraging diners to try a new wine. Crackers is an expression of his experience and talent in the restaurant business. For several years he managed one of the most successful restaurants in Waco, Texas. He then became director of the Food Service Institute at El Centro College, which, with his influence, is now reputed to be one of the best culinary schools in the Southwest.

Gus began Crackers as an experiment: could the personal attitudes toward service and style that he recommended to his students truly be realized in a restaurant? "Yes. We serve quality food at reasonable prices in a relaxing atmosphere. That's what I teach in the classroom, and I think that's what people enjoy about Crackers."

2621 McKinney

ZUCCHINI COINS

2 eggs, beaten
1 (12-ounce) can beer
1½ cups flour
1½ cups cornstarch
¼ teaspoon salt
¼ teaspoon white pepper
½ teaspoon baking powder
3 large zucchini
Bread crumbs
Oil for deep-frying

1. Mix together the eggs, beer, flour, cornstarch, salt, pepper, and baking powder to form a smooth batter.
2. Slice the zucchini ¼ inch thick. Dip first into the batter, then coat with the bread crumbs.
3. Deep-fry in hot cooking oil, turning once, until golden brown.
4. Remove and drain. Serve while hot.

CREAM OF MUSHROOM SOUP

½ pound fresh mushrooms,
   chopped
1 cup chopped onions
6 tablespoons butter
¾ cup flour
1½ quarts Chicken Stock
   (see index)

1 cup whipping cream
Salt
White pepper
Dash of cayenne pepper
CHEESE CRACKERS

1. Sauté the mushrooms and onions in butter until onions are clear, not brown.
2. Add the flour and cook the roux 5 or 6 minutes over low heat, being careful not to let it brown.
3. Add the chicken stock and stir until well blended and the soup is creamy.
4. Stir the whipping cream into the soup. Season with salt, pepper, and cayenne to taste. Continue to cook until the boiling point is reached. Remove immediately from heat.
5. Serve hot with Cheese Crackers.

CHEESE CRACKERS

½ pound butter
½ pound cheddar cheese,
   grated
2 cups flour

¼ teaspoon cayenne pepper
½ teaspoon salt
¼ teaspoon white pepper

1. Preheat oven to 400°.
2. Mix the butter and grated cheese until fluffy.
3. Add the flour and seasonings. Mix well and place in a pastry bag with a plain tip.
4. Pipe circles of dough onto an ungreased cookie sheet. Bake in preheated oven about 10 to 15 minutes.

DINNER SALAD, CRACKERS STYLE

½ head iceberg lettuce
½ head romaine lettuce
½ head leaf lettuce
½ cup sliced carrot rounds
½ cup shredded red cabbage

BLUE CHEESE DRESSING
1 hard-cooked egg, grated
Cherry tomatoes
Bread sticks

1. Wash and dry the salad greens. Break into bite-size pieces and place in a mixing bowl.
2. Add the carrot rounds and shredded cabbage.
3. Toss gently with Blue Cheese Dressing.
4. Garnish with grated egg and cherry tomatoes. Serve on chilled individual salad plates, accompanied by bread sticks.

BLUE CHEESE DRESSING

½ cup mayonnaise
¼ pound blue cheese,
    crumbled
½ cup sour cream

Dash of garlic powder
½ cup buttermilk
½ teaspoon red wine vinegar

Mix all ingredients together thoroughly. Refrigerate until chilled.

BEEF BURGUNDY

2 *pounds beef, cut into 1½"*
  cubes
1 *cup sliced mushrooms*
½ *cup chopped onions*
2 *cups burgundy*
2 *cups Brown Sauce (see*
  index)

⅛ *teaspoon garlic powder*
⅛ *teaspoon pepper*
½ *teaspoon ground thyme*
½ *teaspoon salt*
  REAMES NOODLES

1. Preheat oven to 350°.
2. Arrange the beef, mushrooms, and onions in an ovenproof casserole.
3. Combine the wine and brown sauce. Add the spices and salt, stir well, and pour over the ingredients in the casserole.
4. Cover and bake in preheated oven for 1 hour, or until the beef is tender. Serve with Reames Noodles.

REAMES NOODLES

2 *teaspoons salt*
10 *ounces Reames frozen*
   noodles

4 *tablespoons butter, melted*
1 *teaspoon poppy seeds*
¼ *teaspoon nutmeg*

1. Bring 5 cups water and the salt to a boil in a large saucepan. Add the noodles and cook 20 minutes.
2. Drain and rinse with hot water to remove excess starch; drain thoroughly.
3. Sauté the noodles briefly in melted butter.
4. Sprinkle with poppy seeds and nutmeg; stir gently. Serve while hot.

BROILER TOMATOES

4 large, firm tomatoes	1 teaspoon oregano
1 cup seasoned bread crumbs	¼ teaspoon salt
2 tablespoons butter, melted	¼ teaspoon pepper

1. Cut the tomatoes in half and trim ends so they will set level.
2. Preheat broiler.
3. Combine the remaining ingredients; spoon the mixture on top of the tomato halves.
4. Place under broiler until browned. Serve immediately.

BREAD PUDDING WITH BRANDY SAUCE

5 slices white bread, cut
into cubes
2½ cups whole milk
½ cup whipping cream
3 eggs, beaten
¾ cup sugar

1 teaspoon cinnamon
½ teaspoon vanilla extract
¼ cup raisins
1 tablespoon butter, melted
BRANDY SAUCE

1. Soak the bread cubes in the combined milk and cream for 20 minutes.
2. Preheat oven to 350°. Butter a 1½-quart casserole.
3. Add the remaining ingredients to the bread mixture and mix well. Turn into the prepared casserole and set in a shallow pan containing hot water. Bake in preheated oven for 1 hour. Serve with Brandy Sauce.

BRANDY SAUCE

3 egg yolks
¾ cup sugar
1½ cups whole milk

1 tablespoon cornstarch
1 teaspoon vanilla extract
1½ ounces brandy or rum

1. Beat the egg yolks and sugar until thickened and pale.
2. Heat the milk. Stir a small amount into the egg mixture, then return all to milk, stirring constantly.
3. Dissolve the cornstarch in ¼ cup water and stir into the hot mixture. Continue heating and stirring until the sauce is thick and smooth.
4. Remove from heat; stir in the vanilla and brandy.

ROYAL STREET COFFEE

Per serving—

¾ cup black coffee	Whipped cream
2 tablespoons amaretto	Nutmeg
1 tablespoon Kahlua	

1. Pour the coffee into a cup. Add the amaretto and Kahlua, stirring briefly.
2. Top with whipped cream and a sprinkle of nutmeg.

L'Entrecote

Dinner for Four

Caviar Beluga Malossol au Naturel

Soupe à l'Oignon Gratinée

Anatole Salad
with
Garganzola Dressing

Filet Mignon en Chevreuil

Wild Rice L'Entrecote

Poached Yellow Delicious Apples
with
Chestnut Purée

Soufflé Rothschild

Wine:
With the Filet—Richebourg

Randy L. Gantenbin, Executive Director, Food and Beverage
Howard Smulo, Chef

L'ENTRECOTE

*G*uests dine elegantly at L'Entrecote. They look out onto the park-like setting of Atrium I of Loew's Anatole Dallas from an interior which is softly lit by hundreds of lights, and all the while are soothed by subdued strains of harp music. Equally important, this Continental restaurant provides them with superb gourmet French cuisine presented with impeccable service.

Only extremely high-quality ingredients are used at L'Entrecote: choice dry-aged beef, the freshest fruits and vegetables, the finest of sauces and butters, and the best Colombian coffees. Exquisite hors d'oeuvres begin the meal, followed by a choice of one of twenty-five main courses including such gustatory pleasures as Steak à la Biarritz, Roast Duckling with Pears and Almonds and Williamin Brandy, and Braised Pheasant in Salmis Sauce with Foie Gras and Cognac. The final course of the meal includes soufflés, sherbets, pastries, espresso and anisette, and as a final touch, white and dark chocolate-covered fruits. Chef Howard Smulo supervises a kitchen dedicated to the very finest standards of cuisine in a restaurant dedicated to the very finest standards of dining.

Loew's Anatole-Dallas
2201 Stemmons Freeway North

CAVIAR BELUGA MALOSSOL AU NATUREL

2 ounces Beluga Malossol
  caviar, well chilled

8 BLINIS

1 cup sour cream

1 cup cornichons

4 hard-cooked egg yolks,
  chopped

2 hard-cooked egg whites,
  chopped

2 tablespoons capers

¼ cup chopped Belgian
  onions

Serve the caviar in a glass bowl centered on a silver relish tray, surrounded by the Blinis and chilled condiments. Each person receives a small plate and serves himself Blini, caviar, and condiments of his choosing.

Serve with small glasses of well-chilled Stolichnaya vodka. The vodka can be put in the freezer until thoroughly chilled.

BLINIS

1 cup buckwheat flour

⅛ teaspoon baking soda

¼ teaspoon salt

¼ teaspoon baking powder

⅛ teaspoon white pepper

1 egg, beaten

½ cup milk

1. Preheat a pancake griddle.
2. Mix the dry ingredients together. Blend in the egg and milk.
3. Ladle onto the hot pancake griddle and cook, turning once, until done. The finished blini should be about 4 inches in diameter.

SOUPE A L'OIGNON GRATINÉE

4 tablespoons butter	1 quart beef consommé
2 large white Bermuda onions, thinly sliced	4 toasted bread croutons, 2½" diameter
3 ounces dry sherry	4 thin slices Gruyère cheese

1. Melt the butter in a 1½-quart saucepan and sauté the onions until they begin to color.
2. Add the sherry and cook 2 minutes.
3. Add the beef consommé and simmer 30 minutes.
4. At serving time, preheat oven to 400°. Ladle the soup into 8-ounce ovenproof crocks. Float a crouton on top of each and cover with a slice of Gruyère.
5. Bake in preheated oven until the cheese is melted and golden brown. Serve while hot.

ANATOLE SALAD

½ head romaine lettuce
1 head limestone lettuce
4 leaves Belgian endive
4 leaves spinach
4 sprigs watercress
2 medium-size avocados,
   peeled and sliced into
   6 wedges each

¼ pound cooked lump
   crabmeat
8 medium-size cocktail
   shrimp, boiled, peeled,
   and deveined
GARGANZOLA DRESSING

1. Clean the greens thoroughly. Tear the lettuce, endive, and spinach into bite-size pieces and toss together in a salad bowl.
2. Divide the greens onto four chilled salad plates; top each salad with a sprig of watercress, 3 avocado wedges, an ounce of crabmeat, and 2 shrimp.
3. Top with Garganzola Dressing.

GARGANZOLA DRESSING

2 cups heavy mayonnaise
2 ounces Roquefort cheese
⅓ cup lemon juice
1 teaspoon salt
¼ teaspoon garlic salt
1½ teaspoons white pepper
10 sprigs parsley, very
   finely chopped

2 tablespoons very finely
   chopped chives
2 tablespoons puréed
   shallots
1 cup white wine vinegar

1. Combine the mayonnaise, Roquefort, and lemon juice in a blender. Add the salt, garlic salt, pepper, parsley, chives, and shallots. Blend at low speed.
2. Add the vinegar very slowly while continuing to blend at low speed. Chill before serving.

FILET MIGNON EN CHEVREUIL

2 cups red wine vinegar
½ teaspoon freshly cracked
   pepper
2 sprigs parsley
¼ teaspoon thyme
½ carrot, sliced in thin
   rounds

½ stalk celery, chopped
1 small Spanish onion,
   chopped
4 (7-ounce) beef filets
½ pound butter, clarified
   CHEVREUIL SAUCE

1. An hour and a half before serving time, prepare a marinade by combining the vinegar, pepper, parsley, thyme, carrot, celery, and onion.
2. Place the filets in a glass or plastic container and pour the marinade over to cover. Marinate 1 hour, turning once if liquid does not cover.
3. Remove the steaks from the marinade; strain and reserve marinade for sauce.
4. Warm the butter in a skillet. When quite hot but not yet smoking, sauté the filets, turning once or twice, until of desired degree of doneness.
5. Place on dinner plates and slice each filet diagonally into four or five pieces. Top each serving with 1 tablespoon Chevreuil Sauce.

CHEVREUIL SAUCE

⅓ cup strained marinade,
   reserved from Filet
   Mignon recipe
1½ teaspoons finely chopped
   shallots

1 teaspoon lingonberry jelly
1 cup Brown Sauce (see
   index)

Combine all ingredients in a small saucepan and simmer on low heat for 5 minutes.

Lingonberry jelly is available at gourmet specialty shops if you have difficulty finding it at your grocery store.

WILD RICE L'ENTRECOTE

⅓ cup salad oil	1 teaspoon salt
2 cups wild rice	¼ teaspoon white pepper
1½ teaspoons finely chopped shallots	4 strips crisp lean bacon, diced
¼ teaspoon thyme	¼ cup brandy

1. Preheat oven to 400°.
2. Heat the oil in an ovenproof skillet and sauté the wild rice and shallots until the shallots become translucent. Add the thyme, salt, and white pepper and sauté over medium heat 5 minutes.
3. Add 2 cups water. When it comes to a boil, move the skillet to preheated oven and bake 15 minutes.
4. Return the skillet to range top over medium heat. Stir in bacon.
5. Pour on the brandy; when it is warmed and begins to release its fumes, ignite with a match and let it flame. Serve while hot.

POACHED YELLOW DELICIOUS APPLES

2 *yellow Delicious apples*
2 *tablespoons lemon juice*
⅓ *cup sugar*

1 *tablespoon white wine*
   vinegar
CHESTNUT PURÉE

1. Preheat oven to 350°.
2. Peel, core, and slice each apple in half horizontally.
3. Combine 1 quart boiling water, the lemon juice, sugar, and vinegar in a saucepan; boil the apples in this mixture 5 minutes. Remove and drain.
4. Stuff the drained apples with Chestnut Purée.
5. Bake in preheated oven 10 minutes. May be served warm from the oven or chilled.

CHESTNUT PURÉE

3 *ounces canned chestnut*
   purée

½ *cup mashed potatoes*

Stir the purée and potatoes together until a smooth consistency is reached.

SOUFFLÉ ROTHSCHILD

1 pint fresh strawberries, sliced	Granulated sugar
½ fresh pineapple, peeled, cored, and diced	4 egg whites
Butter	1 (3¾-ounce) package instant vanilla pudding mix
	¾ cup maraschino liqueur

1. Combine the fruits and set aside for the flavors to marry.
2. Preheat oven to 350°. Butter four individual 4-inch soufflé dishes and sprinkle the bottoms with sugar; set aside.
3. Beat the egg whites until stiff.
4. Stir the pudding mix and liqueur together and carefully fold into the egg whites.
5. Ladle 2 to 3 ounces of soufflé mixture into each soufflé dish. Add some fresh fruit mixture and top with additional soufflé base.
6. Bake in preheated oven 15 to 20 minutes, or until golden brown.

Ewald's

Dinner for Four

Shrimp du Chef

White Asparagus Salad

Veal Steak au Moulin

Spätzli

Tomato Stuffed with Creamed Spinach

Fresh Strawberries Romanoff

Wine:
Vouvray, Château Moncoutour

Ewald Scholz, Owner & Chef

*D*iners get special treatment, and feel special when they visit Ewald's, as if they are in a friend's home. As so they should, for Owner and Chef Ewald Scholz strives to keep his successful restaurant small and intimate. "It is very necessary to be in control of the many aspects of a restaurant. I would not be able to do this in a larger establishment, and I feel this personal attention is very important." This personal attention is given in numerous ways, in the attentive service provided, for example, or in the care with which dishes are planned and prepared. A guest can additionally enjoy strolling to the back of the restaurant after placing his order to watch the chefs at work behind a long window.

Ewald's talents have been recognized by more people than just loyal Dallas patrons. He is the recipient of a gold medal at the exposition of International Culinary Art in New York, as well as of many other honors, and is a member of the Academy of Chefs and Les Amis d'Escoffier Society. These distinctions are are well earned and, to the delight of both natives and visitors to Dallas, in full view at Ewald's.

5415 West Lovers Lane

SHRIMP DU CHEF

1 tablespoon butter
1 tablespoon finely chopped
   onion
½ teaspoon finely chopped
   garlic
20 peeled and deveined
   cooked shrimp
2 cups minced fresh
   mushrooms

Juice of ½ lemon
⅓ cup Madeira
½ cup BROWN SAUCE
1 tablespoon finely chopped
   parsley
Salt
White pepper to taste
4 lemon wedges
4 sprigs parsley

1. Melt the butter in a skillet. Sauté the onions and garlic until the onions are translucent.
2. Add the shrimp, mushrooms, and lemon juice and cook 2 minutes.
3. Add the Madeira, then the Brown Sauce, parsley, salt, and white pepper. Reduce 1 minute.
4. Arrange 5 shrimp in each of four coquille shells. Pour the sauce over.
5. Garnish with lemon and parsley.

Serve with French bread as a hot appetizer.

BROWN SAUCE

1½ teaspoons butter, melted
1½ teaspoons all-purpose flour

½ cup Beef Stock (see index)

1. Combine the butter and flour in a saucepan; cook, stirring constantly, for 5 minutes.
2. Stir in the stock. Cook and stir until smooth and thickened.

A short-cut for brown sauce can be made using a concentrated beef base—such as Bovril—and roux and water.

WHITE ASPARAGUS SALAD

1 (17-ounce) can white
  asparagus
  Boston lettuce leaves,
  washed
2 tomatoes, cut in wedges

2 lemons, cut in wedges
2 hard-cooked eggs, cut
  in wedges
  Parsley
  SAUCE VINAIGRETTE

1. Arrange the asparagus on salad plates, preferably of glass.
2. Arrange attractively on top: the lettuce leaves, tomato, lemon, and
   egg wedges, and parsley. Top with Sauce Vinaigrette.

*You may substitute hearts of palm for the asparagus, or use a combination of
the two.*

SAUCE VINAIGRETTE

1⅓ cups vegetable oil
⅔ cup olive oil
1 tablespoon chopped dill
  pickles
½ tablespoon chopped onions
1 hard-cooked egg, chopped
1 teaspoon chopped capers
1 teaspoon chopped parsley

½ teaspoon dry English
  mustard
⅓ cup cider vinegar
  Salt and pepper to taste
  Dash of Worcestershire
  sauce
Juice of 1 lemon

Blend all ingredients.

VEAL STEAK AU MOULIN

8 (2½-ounce) veal tenderloin
  medallions
  Salt
  White pepper
  Flour
2 eggs, beaten
1½ tablespoons clarified
  butter
½ pound fresh mushrooms,
  sliced

1 tablespoon chopped onions
1 tablespoon chopped parsley
  Juice of ½ lemon
¼ cup cognac
⅓ cup dry white wine
1 cup heavy cream
  Parsley sprigs

1. Lightly flatten the veal medallions.
2. Season with salt and white pepper.
3. Dredge in flour and dip in the beaten egg to coat. Sauté in preheated clarified butter about 3 minutes on each side. After turning the medallions, add the sliced mushrooms, onions, and parsley. Simmer a few minutes.
4. Add the lemon juice and cognac; flame the cognac.
5. Add the wine and cream. Simmer about 2 minutes.
6. Remove the veal and arrange on a serving platter. Reduce the sauce a little longer to desired thickness. Taste for seasoning and pour over the veal. Decorate the platter with fresh parsley sprigs.

SPÄTZLI
German-type Homemade Noodles

½ pound all-purpose flour
½ cup milk
¼ cup cold water
2 whole eggs
Dash of nutmeg

Dash of yellow food
    coloring (optional)
Clarified butter
Salt and white pepper
    to taste

1. Sift the flour into a bowl.
2. Add the remaining ingredients except the clarified butter, salt, and white pepper. Beat by hand until bubbles appear. Let rest 30 minutes.
3. Force the dough through a colander into a large pot of boiling water. Simmer until the spätzli come to the surface.
4. Remove with a skimmer directly into a bowl of ice water. When cold, drain completely.
5. When ready to serve, sauté in clarified butter and season with salt and white pepper.

This is an excellent dish to serve with veal, chicken, roast, etc. for variety.

Spätzle machines can be purchased at gourmet stores and are easier to use.

TOMATO STUFFED WITH CREAMED SPINACH

2 *medium-size ripe*   1 *cup creamed or sautéed*
   tomatoes   *spinach*
   Butter   *Grated Parmesan cheese*
   Salt and pepper to taste

1. Preheat oven to 350°.
2. Cut the tomatoes in half. Arrange on a buttered pie pan.
3. Season with salt and pepper and top with the spinach. Sprinkle with a little Parmesan cheese and melted butter.
4. Bake in preheated oven 8 to 10 minutes.

FRESH STRAWBERRIES ROMANOFF

2 *pints fresh strawberries*   *Vanilla ice cream*
2 *tablespoons white or*   *(optional)*
   brown sugar   1 *cup sweetened whipped*
½ *cup Grand Marnier*   *cream*
   liqueur

1. Wash and hull the strawberries.
2. Combine the sugar and Grand Marnier. Marinate the strawberries in the mixture for about 15 minutes.
3. Serve in a compote dish, over ice cream if desired.
4. Garnish with whipped cream.

THE FORBIDDEN CITY

Dinner for Four

Spinach-Mushroom Soup

Szechuan Chicken

Beef with Green Onions

Shrimp with Cashews

Fried Bananas

Wine:

Wang Fu

Henry Ho, Owner

Yao-Hwa Chuang, Chef

*O*wner Henry Ho credits the naming of Forbidden City restaurant to his wife, whose grandparents lived in the Ch'ing Palace—the Forbidden City—from 1889 to 1911. Besides honoring her ancestors, this choice of name aptly describes the restaurant. In an elegant, imperial atmosphere, Forbidden City features traditional and exquisite Mandarin and Hunan cuisine of the Ch'ing dynasty.

Henry and his staff, particularly Chef Yao-Hwa Chuang, are dedicated to the belief that fine food should intrigue all of the senses. They prepare the individual foods with the most careful attention to subtlety of taste and smell. When arranged on a serving platter, these dishes further create a complicated and delightful variety of contrasting colors, shapes, and textures. Many surprises like these await a first-time visitor to Forbidden City, and as the returning patrons happily know, they await each time one dines at Forbidden City.

5290 Belt Line Road, Suite 144
Addison

SPINACH-MUSHROOM SOUP

1 quart Chicken Stock (see index)
½ pound fresh spinach, washed and chopped
¼ pound fresh mushrooms, sliced
3 (3") squares tofu, cut into ¼" strips
2 eggs, lightly beaten

½ teaspoon salt
½ teaspoon sugar
1 tablespoon cooking sherry
1 tablespoon cornstarch
¼ cup cool water
1 teaspoon sesame oil
2 tablespoons finely chopped parsley

1. Heat the chicken stock to boiling. Add the spinach, mushrooms, and tofu and cook 5 minutes.
2. Swirl in the beaten eggs. Add the salt, sugar, and sherry.
3. Dissolve the cornstarch in the water; stir in the sesame oil and add this mixture to the hot soup, stirring in a circular motion.
4. Pour into a serving bowl and dot the center with the parsley. Serve hot.

Serve with crisp noodles in a side dish.

SZECHUAN CHICKEN

1 egg, lightly beaten	*2 teaspoons sugar*
1 tablespoon plus 2 tea-	*1 teaspoon cooking sherry*
spoons cornstarch	*½ cup Chicken Stock (see*
1 tablespoon salad oil	*index)*
1 pound boned chicken	*Chinese hot oil to taste*
breasts, cut into 1" pieces	*2 tablespoons finely chopped*
5 cups soybean oil	*onion greens*
1 cup finely chopped green	*White pepper to taste*
cabbage	*2 tablespoons cool water*
1 teaspoon finely chopped	*2 teaspoons sesame oil*
garlic	*½ cup roasted peanuts*
2 teaspoons salt	

1. Combine the egg, 1 tablespoon cornstarch, and salad oil to form a marinade. Coat the chicken pieces; allow to marinate for 20 minutes.

2. Heat the soybean oil to 360° in a frying pan or wok and deep-fry the chicken and cabbage until the chicken turns white. Remove and set aside.

3. Drain all but 2 tablespoons of the oil from the pan; add the garlic and stir while frying until lightly browned. Add the salt, sugar, sherry, chicken stock, and Chinese hot oil to taste (be careful—the oil can be very hot).

4. Return the chicken and cabbage to the pan. Add the onion greens and white pepper to taste.

5. Dissolve the remaining 2 teaspoons cornstarch in the water; stir in the sesame oil and add to the mixture in the pan. Add the peanuts and stir to combine well.

6. Transfer to a serving platter and serve hot with steamed rice.

Chinese hot oil is available at Oriental grocery stores.

BEEF WITH GREEN ONIONS

½ pound beef flank steak
1 egg, lightly beaten
1 tablespoon cornstarch
1 tablespoon salad oil
2 cups soybean oil
6 green onions with tops,
    sliced into 2" lengths

1 tablespoon soy sauce
1 tablespoon hoisin sauce
1 teaspoon sugar
1 teaspoon sesame oil
White pepper to taste

1. Cut the beef lengthwise into 3-inch strips, then crosswise into ⅛-inch slices. (This is easily done if the meat is partially frozen.)
2. Combine the egg, cornstarch, and salad oil to form a marinade. Coat the beef slices; allow to marinate for 15 minutes.
3. Heat the soybean oil to 360° in a frying pan or wok and deep-fry the beef until browned. Remove and set aside.
4. Drain all but 2 tablespoons of the oil from the pan. Return the beef to the pan and add the green onions.
5. Add the soy sauce, hoisin sauce, sugar, and sesame oil and stir together with the beef. Add white pepper to taste. Transfer to a serving platter and serve hot with steamed rice.

SHRIMP WITH CASHEWS

1 egg white, lightly beaten
1 tablespoon plus 2 tea-
    spoons cornstarch
1 tablespoon salad oil
½ pound fresh shrimp,
    shelled and deveined
2 cups soybean oil
1 teaspoon finely chopped
    garlic
1 teaspoon sherry

½ cup Chicken Stock (see
    index)
2 teaspoons salt
1 tablespoon sugar
2 tablespoons cool water
1 teaspoon sesame oil
½ cup coarsely chopped
    cashews
White pepper to taste

1. Combine the egg white, 1 tablespoon cornstarch, and the salad oil to form a marinade. Coat the shrimp; allow to marinate 20 minutes.

2. Heat the soybean oil to 360° in a frying pan or wok and deep-fry the shrimp 1 minute or until pink. Do not overcook. Remove and set aside.

3. Drain all but 2 tablespoons of the oil from the pan; add the garlic and stir while frying until lightly browned. Add the sherry, chicken stock, salt, and sugar.

4. Dissolve the remaining 2 teaspoons cornstarch in the cool water; stir in the sesame oil and add this to the mixture in the pan. Boil 1 minute.

5. Return the shrimp to the pan. Add the cashews and stir-fry just long enough to coat with the sauce. Add white pepper to taste. Transfer to a serving platter and serve hot with steamed rice.

FRIED BANANAS

4 bananas	1 egg, lightly beaten
Red bean paste	5 cups soybean oil
¼ cup cornstarch	¼ cup sugar
¾ cup flour	2 tablespoons ground peanuts

1. Slice each banana in half lengthwise. Spread bean paste over each cut surface and replace the other half, restoring the original shape.
2. Combine the cornstarch, flour, egg, and enough water to form a creamy batter; coat each re-formed banana with the batter.
3. Heat the oil to 360° in a frying pan or wok. Add the bananas and deep-fry until golden brown. Remove from the oil and drain on paper toweling.
4. Combine the sugar and ground peanuts; coat the fried bananas with this mixture. Serve while hot.

Red bean paste is available at Oriental grocery stores.

French Room

Dinner for Four

Gratin de Moules aux Épinards

Salade d'Endives et Cresson

Tournedos à la Graine de Moutarde

Mousse de Légumes

Feuilleté Chaud aux Framboises, Sauce Caramel

Wine:
With the Mussels—H.M.R. Pinot Chardonnay
With the Tournedos—Gevrey-Chambertin

Jean Marc Dizard, Food and Beverage Director
Michel Cornu, Executive Chef

The ambiance of the newly restored Adolphus Hotel is one of Old World elegance, and guests of the French Room, one of its three dining facilities, can easily imagine themselves in the Palace of Versailles. From top to bottom, the restaurant is a breathtaking palette of brilliance and intricacy. Two hand-blown chandeliers of seventeenth-century design highlight the rococo murals painted on the high arched ceilings. Ornate mouldings and sconces dazzle the eye, as does the carpet hand-made in Hong Kong. Period objects, including silver, crystal, china, and linens, complete the opulent furnishings.

To complement the elegant and extravagant decor of the French Room, the menu offers a spectacular variety of nouvelle and classical cuisine artfully prepared by internationally renowned professionals. Consultant to the French Room is one of the world's most celebrated chefs, Jean Banchet, whose Le Français restaurant outside Chicago is consistently rated among the best of American restaurants. He assisted in developing the cuisine at the French Room and in training the kitchen staff, and he returns to the hotel on a continuing basis.

Open for dinner only, the exclusive French Room promises a guest an evening of incomparably fine dining.

Adolphus Hotel
1321 Commerce

GRATIN DE MOULES AUX ÉPINARDS

5 pounds fresh mussels
   in shells
2 cups dry white wine
1 cup whipping cream
1 cup HOLLANDAISE SAUCE

1 cup whipped cream
3 tablespoons butter
1 pound fresh spinach,
   washed and chopped

1. Steam the mussels in white wine for 3 minutes or until the shells open. Remove from the pan. Shell the mussels and reserve the pan liquid.
2. Strain the pan liquid through a fine cloth; bring to a boil and reduce to ½ cup. Add the whipping cream and boil to reduce slightly. Remove from heat. Allow the mixture to cool until warm.
3. Stir in the Hollandaise Sauce. Carefully fold in the whipped cream until smooth. Set aside.
4. Melt the butter in a large sauté pan over high heat. Add the spinach and sauté until just cooked. Divide evenly into four cassolettes.
5. Divide the cooked mussels over the spinach. Pour the sauce over to fill the cassolettes. Place under a hot broiler to glaze the sauce, taking care not to burn it.

HOLLANDAISE SAUCE

3 egg yolks
1 tablespoon water
½ pound butter, at room
   temperature

1½ teaspoons lemon juice
Salt
White pepper

1. Combine the egg yolks and water in the top of a double boiler over hot but not boiling water. Beat the mixture briskly with a wire whisk until fluffy and thick enough to hold a ribbon for a few seconds.
2. Gradually add one-third of the butter and whisk until the mixture thickens slightly.
3. Add another third of the butter and whisk briskly. Add the remaining butter, whisking until fairly thick.
4. Season with the lemon juice, salt, and white pepper and whisk until combined. Use immediately.

SALADE D'ENDIVES ET CRESSON

3 *cups watercress*
VINAIGRETTE DRESSING

3 *Belgian endives, leaves*
separated

1. Wash the watercress thoroughly. Remove the stems and discard. Place in a bowl; add Vinaigrette Dressing to coat and toss well.
2. Place the endive leaves in a separate bowl and toss with more dressing.
3. Place the watercress in the middle of a serving plate. Arrange the endive leaves around to resemble the petals of a flower. Serve chilled.

VINAIGRETTE DRESSING

¾ *cup walnut oil*
¼ *cup Xérès vinegar*

Salt and pepper to taste

Combine all ingredients thoroughly and chill.

TOURNEDOS A LA GRAINE DE MOUTARDE

4 *teaspoons butter*
4 *(9-ounce) filets mignons*
1½ *cups dry white wine*
2 *cups cream*
1 *teaspoon whole mustard*
    seeds
1½ *teaspoons prepared Dijon*
    mustard

⅓ *cup finely chopped green*
    onions
4 *teaspoons finely chopped*
    shallots
Salt and pepper to taste

1. Melt the butter in a skillet and sauté the filets over high heat, turning several times to brown all over. Cook to desired degree of doneness. Set aside on a serving platter; keep warm.
2. Add the white wine to the skillet and stir to deglaze; cook over high heat to reduce liquid by one-half.
3. Add the cream and reduce a few minutes more.
4. Add the mustard seeds, prepared mustard, green onions, shallots, and salt and pepper and stir well.
5. Cover the filets with the sauce and serve.

MOUSSE DE LÉGUMES

⅓ pound carrots, peeled
 and coarsely chopped
⅓ pound summer squash,
 cut in thick slices
⅓ pound turnips, coarsely
 chopped

1 cup whipping cream
2 eggs, lightly beaten
 Salt and pepper to taste

1. In separate saucepans, boil the carrots, squash, and turnips until very well done and tender. Drain.
2. Purée each batch of vegetables and combine until smooth.
3. Preheat oven to 350°.
4. Heat the cream to the boiling point and stir into the vegetable mixture.
5. Fold in the beaten eggs. Season with salt and pepper.
6. Pour into individual casseroles, place in a deep baking pan partially filled with hot water, and bake in preheated oven until the mousse has set, approximately 20 minutes. Serve warm.

FEUILLETÉ CHAUD AUX FRAMBOISES, SAUCE CARAMEL

½ sheet puff pastry dough
1 cup powdered sugar,
  or as needed
2 cups ORANGE CRÈME
  PÂTISSIÈRE

1 cup fresh raspberries
SAUCE CARAMEL

1. Roll the puff pastry into a rectangle approximately 6 inches by 12 inches by ⅛ inch thick. Place on a baking sheet lined with parchment paper. Prick the entire surface with a fork to prevent bubbles from forming when baking. Let rest 1 hour.

2. Preheat oven to 400°. Bake the dough for 15 minutes or until puffed and golden brown. Remove from the baking sheet and cool on a cooling rack, bottom side up. Preheat broiler.

3. When the pastry is cool, cut into eight 3-inch by 3-inch squares. Sprinkle each square with a generous amount of powdered sugar and place under the broiler until the sugar melts into a glaze. Do not burn.

4. Place four of the squares on individual dessert plates. Mound each with a large portion of Crème Pâtissière. Place equal amounts of the whole raspberries on the cream, top with more cream, and finally place the remaining pastry squares on top. Sprinkle with more powdered sugar. Drizzle Sauce Caramel around.

5. Place under broiler again briefly to glaze the sugar and heat the caramel. Serve immediately.

Note: Puff pastry dough is available frozen in a four-sheet, 10-inch by 13-inch package at specialty food stores.

Use fresh strawberries if raspberries are not in season.

ORANGE CRÈME PÂTISSIÈRE

4 egg yolks
⅔ cup granulated sugar
2 tablespoons cake flour
2 tablespoons cornstarch
2 cups milk

1 teaspoon vanilla extract
2 tablespoons Grand Marnier
1 teaspoon grated orange peel
½ cup whipping cream

1. Beat the egg yolks and sugar together until thick and creamy. Add the flour and cornstarch while continuing to beat.
2. Bring the milk to a boil and slowly beat into the egg mixture.
3. Place the mixture over moderate heat and bring to a boil, stirring constantly. Cook until very thick, about 5 minutes. Remove from heat.
4. Stir in the vanilla extract, Grand Marnier, and orange peel. Allow to cool.
5. Whip the cream until very stiff. Fold into the custard mixture. Refrigerate until ready to use.

SAUCE CARAMEL

½ cup granulated sugar
2 tablespoons water
1 cup whipping cream, at room temperature

4 tablespoons butter, cut into small pieces

1. Mix the sugar with the water in a heavy saucepan. Cook over medium heat until the sugar forms a syrup. Reduce heat and continue cooking until the syrup turns a caramel color. Remove from heat.
2. Add the cream and mix well.
3. Add the butter a little at a time, stirring until thoroughly blended.

Goldfinger

Dinner for Six

Saganaki Cheese

Greek Salad

Moussaka

String Beans Grecian Style

Galaktoboureko

Wine:

Demestica white

Charles Venis & Nick Avlos, Owners

Nick Avlos, Master Chef

K onstantinos Venetis and Nikos Avlogitos, better known to friends as Charles Venis and Nikos Avlos, have created in their Goldfinger Greek Restaurant and Taverna a restaurant unlike any other. Throughout its ten-year history, Goldfinger has expanded three times, and these expansions are what have made it so captivating. The atmosphere is pleasingly Aegean, established by a delightful cuisine and continuous evening entertainment. Greek folk dancers share the bill with belly dancers, and a Bouzoukia musical group from Athens offers a nice contrast to the more subdued dinner music.

The two partners also cater to a thriving daytime clientele with special luncheons of both Greek and American cuisines. The combination of outstanding food and lively entertainment keeps a steady flow of patrons coming to Goldfinger.

2905 Cridelle

SAGANAKI CHEESE

1½ pounds Kafolotyri or
    Romano cheese
1 pint milk
2 eggs

Flour
Oil for deep-frying
Juice of 2½ lemons

1. Slice the cheese into 1½-inch squares, ½ inch thick. Set aside.
2. In a medium-size bowl, beat together the milk and eggs.
3. Dip the squares of cheese into the milk/egg mixture, then dredge in flour. Place on a tray covered with waxed paper; refrigerate 2 hours.
4. Deep-fry quickly in 425° oil until golden brown. The cheese should be soft on the inside but not melted. Drain on paper towels.
5. Sprinkle with lemon juice and serve while hot.

If the cooking oil is not hot enough, the cheese will melt before it browns. Test if the oil is hot enough by deep-frying a 1-inch cube of bread; it will float to the top in 1 minute if the oil is at the correct temperature.

GREEK SALAD

2 heads romaine
1 tablespoon oregano
1 tablespoon salt
   Freshly ground black
     pepper to taste
½ cup olive oil
½ cup red wine vinegar

2 tomatoes, quartered
1 cucumber, peeled and
   sliced
   Greek olives
½ pound feta cheese, cubed
12 anchovy filets

1. Wash and dry the lettuce and tear or shred into a large bowl.
2. Sprinkle with oregano, salt, and pepper. Add the oil, vinegar, tomatoes, cucumber, olives, and feta cheese; toss thoroughly.
3. Serve on chilled plates, garnished with anchovy filets.

MOUSSAKA

3 medium-size eggplants
Flour
Oil
1 medium-size onion, finely chopped
1 pound ground beef or veal
2 tablespoons butter, melted
Salt and pepper to taste

¼ teaspoon nutmeg
¼ teaspoon allspice
¼ cup dry white wine
½ pound Romano cheese, grated
4 eggs, beaten
1 pint whole milk

1. Peel the eggplant and slice lengthwise ⅜ inch thick.
2. Dredge in flour and fry in hot cooking oil, turning once, until golden brown. Drain and reserve.
3. Sauté the onion and ground meat in butter in a skillet.
4. Add the salt, pepper, nutmeg, and allspice and cook until the onion is clear and the meat is browned.
5. Preheat oven to 350°.
6. Butter a casserole and place one layer of eggplant in the bottom. Spread with a portion of the meat mixture. Sprinkle with the grated Romano. Repeat layering until all ingredients are used.
7. Stir the beaten eggs and milk together and add salt and pepper to taste. Pour the mixture over the casserole ingredients.
8. Bake in preheated oven about ½ hour, or until the top is golden brown and the casserole is firm. Cut into individual portions and serve while hot.

STRING BEANS GRECIAN STYLE

2 pounds fresh or frozen
    string beans
1 teaspoon salt
1 teaspoon olive oil
1 pound butter or margarine
1 large white onion, finely
    chopped

2 fresh tomatoes, peeled
    and chopped
Salt
White pepper
1 tablespoon Lea & Perrins
    Worcestershire sauce

1. Wash and cut the beans for cooking. Place in a saucepan with a small amount of water; add the salt and olive oil. Cook until crisp-tender. Drain and reserve.
2. Melt the butter in a skillet and sauté the onion and tomato until softened.
3. Season with salt and pepper to taste, add the Lea & Perrins, and combine with the beans. Serve while hot.

GALAKTOBOUREKO

This custard dish should be served hot with the syrup at room temperature, so it is necessary to make the syrup first in order to allow time for it to cool adequately.

1 quart milk
2 cups sugar
1 cup simigdali
4 eggs
¼ teaspoon vanilla extract
¼ pound butter plus 4
    tablespoons melted butter

1 teaspoon lemon peel,
    grated
14 fillo leaves
SYRUP

1. Heat the milk and sugar in a saucepan. Bring to a boil and hold ready.
2. In a separate saucepan, mix the simigdali, eggs, and vanilla extract. Add milk, mixing thoroughly. Bring the combined mixture to a boil and remove from heat. Add ¼ pound butter, stirring until melted. Add the lemon peel.
3. Preheat oven to 250°.
4. Butter a small baking dish. Fold two fillo leaves in half. Lay them in the bottom of the pan so that half lies inside, half outside. Repeat procedure on all sides. Lay an additional leaf over the bottom, covering the overlapping leaves.
5. Pour in the custard mixture. Fold fillo flaps over the mixture; lay two more leaves over the top. Brush with melted butter and bake in preheated oven 50 minutes.
6. When ready, glaze the top with Syrup. Cut into squares and serve.

Simigdali is available at Greek groceries or specialty markets.

SYRUP

1 *pound sugar*	5 *whole cloves*
4 *cups water*	*Juice of 1 lemon*
2 *cinnamon sticks*	

1. Combine all ingredients in a saucepan and heat to a boil. When boiling, check a teaspoonful to see if it is sticky and syrupy. If so, remove from heat immediately. Syrup will get too thick if allowed to continue boiling.
2. Set aside and cool to room temperature

The syrup recipe will make more than needed for the Galaktoboureko, but it is not possible to make it in smaller batches without losing some quality. Remaining syrup is delicious served over ice cream.

Dinner for Four

Mushroom Soup

Avocado Salad Turbeville

Breast of Chicken Pappagallo

Coupe Ambassadrice

Wine:

Firestone Chardonnay,
or
Carneros Creek Chardonnay
or
Roudon-Smith Chardonnay

Charlotte Parker & Kathy McDaniel, Owners
Michael Blackwell, Chef

*S*ince its opening in 1972, the Grape has established itself in the Dallas area as a trendsetter. It was, for one, the first local restaurant to specialize in wines. Then, although the original menu was limited, in that it served primarily to complement the extensive wine list, one of its original entrées was another first in Dallas—quiche. Today the menu has been expanded to ambitious levels, and all to the satisfaction of those who seek the unusual in fine dining.

Chef Michael Blackwell is largely responsible for the continued success of the Grape's cuisine. He has an unconventional background, having been self-educated rather than formally schooled. "I taught myself French cuisine with a large gastronomic encyclopedia and by cooking night after night at the Grape," he explains. "My experience is that a cooking school can ruin you—it gives you a big head. All of my training was gained through working with chefs in California and working in private homes."

He ordains that the menu be individualistic and flexible. Although selections always include veal, seafood, chicken, beef, pasta, and the well-known Mushroom Soup, the particular recipes change nightly, depending upon the availability of fresh ingredients and the current popularity of certain dishes. Patrons can always count on an unusual and delightful fare when they dine at the Grape.

2808 Greenville Avenue

MUSHROOM SOUP

4 tablespoons unsalted butter
1 medium-size onion, finely
  chopped
1 pound fresh mushrooms,
  chopped
3 tablespoons all-purpose
  flour

4 cups beef bouillon or
  Beef Stock (see index)
Pinch of white pepper
Pinch of nutmeg
1½ cups whipping cream

1. Melt the butter in a large saucepan; add the onion and sauté over medium-high heat until transparent.
2. Add the mushrooms and cook until tender.
3. Add the flour, stirring constantly.
4. Stir in the beef bouillon and bring to a boil. Season with white pepper and nutmeg.
5. Remove from heat; stir in the cream. Serve immediately.

Note: The mushrooms should be randomly chopped so that there are both large and small pieces.

The secret to this soup is to use very fresh cream and mushrooms.

AVOCADO SALAD TURBEVILLE

1 *head Bibb or butter lettuce*	*DRESSING*
2 *medium-size tomatoes,*	*Toasted sesame seeds*
sliced ½" thick	*Freshly ground pepper*
2 *medium-size avocados,*	*Black olives*
sliced ¼" thick	*Parsley*

Separate the lettuce leaves and arrange on four chilled salad plates. Place the tomato and avocado slices alternately on the lettuce. Top each salad with dressing, sprinkle with sesame seeds and pepper, and garnish with olives and parsley on the side.

DRESSING

2 *tablespoons Dijon mustard*	1¼ *cups vegetable oil*
2 *egg yolks*	½ *teaspoon salt*
¼ *cup white vinegar*	*Pinch of white pepper*

Combine the mustard and egg yolks in a medium-size bowl; beat with a wire whisk until thick. Beat in the vinegar. Alternately add the oil and ¼ cup water, pouring slowly and beating constantly. Season with the salt and white pepper.

Note: To toast sesame seeds, place in an ungreased skillet or pie pan. Bake at 350°, stirring frequently, for 15 minutes or until golden brown.

BREAST OF CHICKEN PAPPAGALLO

4 *(6 to 8-ounce) boned chicken breasts, skinned*	½ *cup sliced fresh mushrooms*
⅓ *cup plus 2 tablespoons all-purpose flour*	2 *cups CHICKEN STOCK (see next page)*
1 *teaspoon salt*	½ *teaspoon oregano*
Pinch of white pepper	¾ *cup dry vermouth*
¼ *pound butter*	1 *cup whipping cream*
2 *tablespoons olive oil*	*Grated Parmesan cheese*

1. Flatten the chicken breasts with the palm of the hand. Combine the ⅓ cup flour, the salt, and white pepper; dust the chicken breasts with the flour mixture.

2. Melt 4 tablespoons butter and the oil in a skillet over medium-high heat. Add the chicken and sauté for 15 minutes or until browned, shaking the pan occasionally to prevent sticking. Remove the chicken from the pan, set aside, and keep warm. Remove and discard one-half the pan drippings, leaving the other half in the pan for preparing the sauce. Set the pan aside.

3. Melt 2 tablespoons butter in another skillet. Add the mushrooms and sauté until done; set aside.

4. Melt the remaining 2 tablespoons butter in a small pan. Add the remaining 2 tablespoons flour and make a roux by cooking, stirring with a wire whisk, for 1 minute. Set aside.

5. Combine the chicken stock and oregano in a saucepan. Bring to a boil and boil 5 minutes. Strain through a fine sieve to remove the oregano. Place the broth in the skillet in which the chicken was cooked and add the vermouth; bring to a boil. Add the roux, beating constantly with a wire whisk until thickened.

6. Remove from heat. Stir in the reserved mushrooms and the cream. Add the chicken breasts, spooning sauce over each to cover. Serve at once; sprinkle each serving with Parmesan cheese.

Orange rice and asparagus or broccoli in lemon or orange butter would nicely accompany this entrée. Serve also with a good French bread and butter.

THE GRAPE

CHICKEN STOCK

1 whole chicken
2 carrots, quartered
1 large onion, quartered
4 ribs celery, coarsely
   chopped
2 bay leaves
2 sprigs parsley

1 teaspoon thyme
Pinch of tarragon
1 clove garlic
Dash of Tabasco sauce
2 teaspoons salt
6 cups water
2 cups white wine (optional)

Combine all the ingredients in a 4 or 6-quart stock pot. Bring to a boil and cook until the chicken falls off the bone very easily, about 45 minutes. Remove the chicken. Strain the broth through a fine sieve and skim the fat off the top of the stock.

This recipe makes 7 to 8 cups stock, but whatever will not be used immediately can be frozen.

COUPE AMBASSADRICE

½ pound amaretti cookies
1 pint fresh strawberries
1 ounce Grand Marnier
¼ cup honey (optional)
4 small white peaches
½ cup whipping cream
   (approximately)

1½ pints cassis sorbet (preferably Häagen-Dazs)
2 kiwi, peeled and sliced ¼" thick
½ pint fresh raspberries
Candied violets
Mint leaves

1. Preheat oven to 350°.
2. Crush the cookies with a rolling pin. Place in a baking pan and bake in preheated oven 15 to 20 minutes or until toasted and browned. Set aside to cool.
3. Combine the strawberries, Grand Marnier, and honey in a food processor. Purée and set aside.
4. Fill a small saucepan two-thirds full of water; bring to a boil. Add the whole peaches and boil 2 minutes. Remove the peaches to a bowl of ice water; let stand 1 minute. Score the peach skin with a knife and remove the peel. Remove the pits from the peaches by inserting an iced-tea spoon or any other slender spoon in the stem end and turning to loosen pit.
5. Combine the cookie crumbs and enough cream to make a stiff paste. Fill each peach with the cookie mixture.
6. Divide the sorbet evenly among four parfait glasses. Make an indentation in each dip of sorbet and set one peach in each dip. Line the sides of each glass with kiwi slices, spoon the puréed strawberries over the peaches, and evenly divide the raspberries among the parfaits. Garnish with candied violets and mint leaves.

Note: Use yellow peaches if white are unavailable. Amaretti cookies can be found at gourmet food shops but can be substituted with homemade almond macaroons. Candied violets may also be found at gourmet shops.

Pirouettes or gaufrettes—French waffle cookies—nicely complement this dessert, as does chocolate or plain cappucino.

Javier's

Dinner for Four

Combination Nachos

Chicken Garbanzo Soup

Filete Albanil

Mango Custard

Café Pierre

Wine:

Châteauneuf-du-Pape, Jaboulet-Vercherre

Javier Gutierrez, Owner

When Javier Gutierrez emigrated with his family to Dallas, he admits that he was "frustrated by what everyone calls 'Mexican food' here. I am from Mexico, and had never eaten any of this." So he opened Javier's, which admirably succeeds in recreating both the cuisine and ambiance of Mexico City.

Many of the basic recipes used in the restaurant come from his mother's private collection. She and the other chefs, however, are not content with the status quo; they constantly experiment to improve the flavors of the dishes. Javier also participates in this process by contributing research he gains through frequent trips to Mexico, as well as by making the ultimate decisions about recipe revisions. He and his staff have managed to lure many of their guests away from selecting tacos and enchiladas to preferring more succulent, tender, and authentic beef, seafood, and chicken dishes.

The furnishings of the restaurant are highlighted by Spanish colonial antiques and festival masks from the Yucatán which set off a large photgraphic mural of the Copper canyon. Together with the food, the decor shows how much Javier has succeeded in meeting his goal: "I have pride in my background and in Mexico . . . I want to give a different image of Mexico City—to show it as I know it."

4912 Cole Avenue

COMBINATION NACHOS

8 corn tortillas, quartered
  Corn oil
½ pound REFRIED BLACK
  BEANS
6 ounces Monterey Jack
  cheese, sliced

GUACAMOLE (see
  next page)
1 cup sour cream
  Sliced jalapeño peppers

1. Deep-fry the tortillas in hot corn oil until crisp; drain.
2. Spread each tortilla chip with beans and top with a slice of cheese.
3. Broil until the cheese melts.
4. Top with Guacamole, sour cream, and jalapeño pepper slices.

REFRIED BLACK BEANS

½ pound dried black turtle
  beans
¼ pound pure lard, heated

Salt to taste

1. Wash the beans. Place in a large pan and add water to cover.
2. Bring just to a boil. Reduce heat and simmer 2 hours or until tender.
   Drain, reserving ½ cup liquid. Mash the beans.
3. Place the lard in a skillet over medium-high heat. When the fat is
   hot, add the mashed beans. Lower heat and fry slowly for 10 minutes, stirring constantly.

To judge when lard is ready for frying, insert a wooden spoon in hot lard. If lard bubbles vigorously around the edges of the spoon, it's hot enough. It must be hot enough that food can be fried without absorbing the flavor of the raw lard.

GUACAMOLE

3 ripe avocados, peeled and
  mashed
1 tomato, chopped
1 onion, chopped
5 fresh serrano peppers,
  chopped

6 sprigs cilantro, chopped
  Juice of ½ lemon
1 teaspoon salt
¼ teaspoon white pepper

1. Combine the first five ingredients, mixing well.
2. Stir in remaining ingredients.

Cilantro is also sold as coriander or Chinese parsley. Serrano chiles are small, about 1½ inches long. They have a smooth, green skin and are round with pointed ends.

CHICKEN GARBANZO SOUP

6 cups Chicken Stock (see index)
½ chicken, cut up
1 tablespoon chicken fat
1 cup water
2 green onions, chopped
½ clove garlic, minced
  Juice of 1 lemon
1 teaspoon salt
  Pinch of ground cloves
2 tablespoons hot sauce

3 tablespoons Worcestershire sauce
  Pinch of white pepper
1 (8-ounce) can garbanzo beans, drained
2 carrots, chopped
½ cup chopped green beans
½ cup peas
1 tomato, peeled and chopped
½ cup cooked rice

1. Combine the first 12 ingredients in a pot and bring just to a boil; simmer 30 minutes.
2. Remove the bones from the chicken. Cut the meat into large pieces and return to the pot.
3. Add remaining ingredients. Simmer 10 to 15 minutes.

Much of the cooking of Mexico was influenced by the French in the sixteenth century. The result was some of the finest dishes anywhere—a mixture of French dishes seasoned with Mexican spices.

FILETE ALBANIL

5 mulato peppers
3 tomatoes, coarsely chopped
2 cloves garlic
1 teaspoon oregano
½ teaspoon white pepper
1½ pounds beef tenderloin, sliced ¼" thick

½ pound fresh mushrooms, sliced
½ cup red wine
1 tablespoon chopped parsley
2 tablespoons butter, melted
1 teaspoon olive oil

1. Remove the stem and core from the peppers. Split open and remove the veins and seeds. Wash in cold running water.
2. Chop the peppers. Soak in 1 cup hot water for 20 minutes.
3. Combine the peppers, soaking water, tomatoes, garlic, oregano, and white pepper in an electric blender and purée.
4. Simmer the tenderloin, mushrooms, pepper purée, wine, and parsley in the butter and oil for 20 minutes.

Note: The seeds of peppers provide the fire. You may prefer to leave a few in.

Mulato peppers have a unique flavor—a little hot, a little sweet.

MANGO CUSTARD

4 *fresh mangos, peeled and*
  sliced
1 *(5⅓-ounce) can*
  evaporated milk

½ *(14-ounce) can sweetened*
  condensed milk
1 *tablespoon amaretto*
  liqueur

1. Combine all ingredients in a mixing bowl. Beat on medium speed of an electric mixer for 5 minutes.
2. Chill thoroughly before serving.

Two 16-ounce cans sliced mangos and ½ cup of the juice may be used instead of fresh mangos.

Javier got this recipe from his mother.

CAFÉ PIERRE

  Sugar
4 *ounces 151-proof rum*
4 *ounces Kahlua*
2 *ounces brandy*

2 *ounces amaretto liqueur*
4 *cups coffee (approximately)*
  Whipped cream

1. Dip the rim of each glass in the rum, and then in the sugar to coat.
2. Add 1 ounce of the rum to each glass, drizzling down the sides without washing off the sugar.
3. Ignite and allow to burn until the sugar melts. Pour out any remaining rum.
4. Add 1 ounce Kahlua, ½ ounce brandy, ½ ounce amaretto, and 1 cup coffee to each glass.
5. Top with about 1½ inches of whipped cream.

Jean-Claude Restaurant

Dinner for Four

Cheese Soufflé

Spinach Salad

Filet de Sole St. Germain

Zucchini Printanière

Strawberry Flambé

Wine:

Mâcon Blanc

Jean-Claude Prevot, Owner & Chef

*J*ean-Claude Prevot moved to Dallas nearly fifteen years ago, and since that time he has become one of the most well-known and highly respected gourmet cooks in the area. His first position was one he held for some time, chef at the Pyramid Room. Following that he taught in cooking schools where his reputation flourished. Former students, those longing to be students, and diners lucky enough to have sampled his dishes, all were delighted at the opening of Jean-Claude Restaurant.

Maintaining a small dining capacity assures the intimacy and attentiveness which his restaurant offers. The galley kitchen opens out into the dining room which allows patrons to watch the master and his staff at work. The menu changes daily, according to what is fresh and in season, so that guests' palates are constantly, and always happily, surprised. A variety of fish is always available depending on what is received fresh from Boston, and other standards include veal, duckling, and rack of lamb. An excellent wine list is a source of pride with Jean-Claude's entire staff, but no less a source of pride is their skill and success at making Jean-Claude Restaurant a favorite choice for those who insist on the best in fine dining.

2404 Cedar Springs

CHEESE SOUFFLÉ

3 tablespoons butter	Nutmeg (optional)
6 tablespoons all-purpose flour	½ cup finely diced Gruyère cheese
1⅓ cups cold milk	½ cup finely diced cheddar cheese
4 egg yolks	6 to 8 egg whites
½ teaspoon salt	Dash of cream of tartar
¼ teaspoon white pepper	

1. Preheat oven to 375°.
2. Butter and flour a 6-cup soufflé dish and set aside.
3. Warm a heavy saucepan over medium heat; add the butter and melt. Add the flour, stirring constantly until the mixture becomes light and soupy.
4. Add the milk all at once. Stir well until the mixture begins to boil.
5. Reduce heat to low. Add the egg yolks one at a time, stirring quickly after each addition.
6. Stir in the salt, pepper, and nutmeg. Stir in the cheeses until melted, then set the pan off the heat.
7. Beat the egg whites and cream of tartar until very fluffy. Mix a small amount into the cooked mixture, then add the remainder, blending with a spoon.
8. Pour into the prepared dish; bake in preheated oven 25 to 30 minutes. Serve immediately.

It is not absolutely necessary to have Gruyère cheese; you can use 1 cup cheddar.

SPINACH SALAD

2 thick slices bacon, chopped	Cracked pepper
10 to 12 ounces fresh spinach	2 tablespoons wine vinegar
Salt	CROUTONS
Freshly ground pepper	

1. Sauté the bacon until crisp. Set the bacon and drippings aside.
2. Sprinkle the spinach with salt, ground pepper, and cracked pepper. Add the vinegar and toss.
3. Pour the bacon and hot drippings over the spinach. Toss. Add the Croutons and serve.

CROUTONS

1 cup small French bread cubes	1 to 2 cloves garlic, mashed
1 tablespoon vegetable oil	¼ cup grated Parmesan cheese

1. Preheat oven to 375°.
2. Place the bread cubes on a cookie sheet, distributing evenly.
3. Combine the oil and garlic and pour over the bread cubes.
4. Bake in preheated oven 10 to 15 minutes, or until browned. Toss once during cooking.
5. Remove from oven and sprinkle with Parmesan cheese while still hot.

FILET DE SOLE ST. GERMAIN

5 double or 10 single fillets of sole
¼ pound butter, clarified
1½ cups fresh bread crumbs

1½ teaspoons salt
½ teaspoon white pepper
½ cup chopped parsley
BÉARNAISE SAUCE

1. Preheat broiler.
2. Dry the fillets with a towel, then coat well with clarified butter.
3. Roll in the bread crumbs, pressing the crumbs into fillets with your hands.
4. Pour the remaining butter into a baking dish. Lay the fillets side by side in the dish. Sprinkle with salt, pepper, and parsley.
5. Placing the pan in the middle of the oven, broil 12 minutes. Serve with Béarnaise Sauce.

BÉARNAISE SAUCE

¼ cup white wine
2 tablespoons tarragon vinegar
1 tablespoon finely chopped shallots
2 white peppercorns, crushed
2 sprigs tarragon, chopped

1 sprig chervil, finely chopped
3 egg yolks, beaten
¼ pound plus 4 tablespoons butter, melted
Salt and pepper to taste

1. Combine the first six ingredients in the top of a double boiler. Cook over direct heat, stirring frequently, until reduced by half. Cool.
2. Place over a pan of hot water. Add the egg yolks and butter alternately, a little at a time, beating briskly and steadily.
3. Season to taste.

Clarifying butter is not difficult. The easiest way is to melt the butter in a dish in the oven. Let it get hot enough that it is just about to fry. The top will be very foamy and the clarified liquid part will be on the bottom. Strain off the foam with a fine-mesh strainer.

ZUCCHINI PRINTANIÈRE

2 carrots	*Thyme*
2 zucchini	½ onion, chopped
Butter	2 cloves garlic, minced
Salt	Olive oil
Pepper	2 tomatoes, sliced

1. Preheat oven to 350°.
2. Cut the carrots and zucchini into sticks. Set the zucchini aside.
3. Place the carrots in a small pan. Add a little butter and season with salt, pepper, and thyme to taste.
4. Add a small amount of water. Cover and cook until crisp-tender.
5. Sauté the onion and garlic in olive oil; season with salt, pepper, and thyme. Remove from the skillet and set aside.
6. In the same skillet, sauté the zucchini quickly over high heat. Season with salt, pepper, and thyme.
7. Layer the carrots, onion mixture, zucchini, and tomatoes in a casserole. Bake in preheated oven for 10 to 15 minutes.

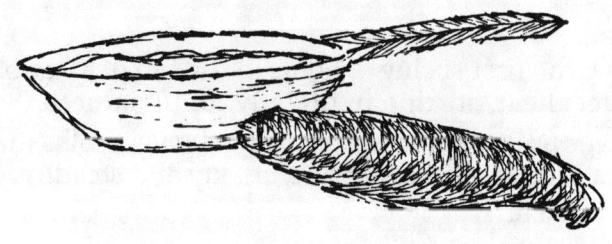

STRAWBERRY FLAMBÉ

2 *tablespoons butter*	2 *pints fresh strawberries*
6 *tablespoons sugar*	½ *cup brandy*
Juice of 1 lemon	4 *scoops vanilla ice cream*

1. Cook the butter and sugar in a skillet until a light brown syrup forms.
2. Blend in the lemon juice.
3. Add strawberries; sauté until tender.
4. Add the brandy and ignite. Cook until the liquid is reduced to desired state.
5. Spoon the strawberry sauce over ice cream and serve.

Mario's

Dinner for Six

Cannelloni Signora Cristine

Insalata Verde

Lasagna Verde Pavarotti

Cannoli alla Siciliana

Wine:

With the Cannelloni—Dolcetto, Pio Caesare

With the Lasagna—Corvo Duca di Salaparuta

Phil Vaccaro, Owner

Jean LaFont, Executive Chef

Antonio Avona, Chef de Cuisine

*M*ario's has a well-established reputation among Dallas restaurants, as do its owners, the Vaccaro family. The reputation is outstanding. The extensive menu features Northern Italian food, but Mario's is much more than just another pasta place. Pasta does play an important role, but not to the exclusion of chicken, seafood, and numerous veal dishes. The large variety and number of appetizers offered suggest how tempting are the non-pasta selections.

Warm deep colors make for an elegant decor which features items from Christine Vaccaro's collection—Venetian glass, porcelain plates, elaborate mirrors. Despite changes in location since its opening in 1945, Mario's has maintained such standards of excellence that the loyalty of its clientele is assured.

135 Turtle Creek Village
Oak Lawn at Blackburn

CANNELLONI SIGNORA CRISTINE

¾ pound fresh spinach
2 tablespoons olive oil
1 cup finely chopped onion
1 teaspoon finely chopped
  garlic
2 tablespoons butter
1 pound pork, ground twice
2 chicken livers
5 tablespoons freshly grated
  Parmesan cheese

½ teaspoon oregano
Salt and freshly ground
  pepper
GREEN PASTA DOUGH
  (see next page)
BÉCHAMEL SAUCE or
  TOMATO SAUCE (see
  next page)

1. Preheat oven to 400°.
2. Cook the spinach in boiling water; drain well, then squeeze out all excess moisture. Chop finely and set aside.
3. Heat the olive oil in a stainless steel skillet. Add the onion and garlic; cook over moderate heat, stirring frequently, until soft. Do not brown.
4. Stir in the spinach. Cook until all moisture has evaporated. Transfer to a large mixing bowl.
5. In the same skillet, melt 1 tablespoon of the butter. Add the pork and brown.
6. Add the onion and spinach mixture; set aside.
7. Melt the remaining butter; add the chicken livers and cook until lightly browned but still pink inside.
8. Chop the livers coarsely and add to the spinach mixture. Add the Parmesan cheese and oregano; mix well. Season with salt and pepper to taste.
9. Spoon the filling lengthwise down the centers of the pasta rectangles. Roll the pasta around the filling to form cylinders. Place in a buttered baking dish. Cover with Béchamel or Tomato Sauce and bake in preheated oven for 20 minutes.

GREEN PASTA DOUGH

4 cups all-purpose flour
3 eggs

1 cup finely chopped and well-drained cooked spinach

1. Sift the flour onto a pastry board. Make a well in the center. Add the eggs and spinach. Work into the dough energetically until it becomes smooth and pliable.
2. Roll the dough paper-thin. Sprinkle lightly with flour to prevent sticking. Cut the dough into 4-inch by 4½-inch rectangles.
3. Drop a few pieces of pasta at a time into boiling water and cook al dente. Drain; cool and dry.

Note: For every pound of pasta, use 6 quarts rapidly boiling water, 2 tablespoons salt, and 2 tablespoons oil for cooking.

Fresh homemade pasta cooks much more quickly than commercial—a few minutes is enough. Always cook pasta "al dente," tender but still a little firm.

BÉCHAMEL SAUCE

4 tablespoons butter
¼ cup all-purpose flour
1 cup milk

1 cup whipping cream
1 teaspoon salt
⅛ teaspoon white pepper

1. In a heavy saucepan, melt the butter over moderate heat. Remove pan from heat; stir in the flour.
2. Add the milk and cream all at once, whisking constantly until the flour partially dissolves. Return pan to high heat; cook, stirring constantly, until the sauce boils and is smooth.
3. Reduce heat and simmer 2 to 3 minutes or until sauce is thick enough to heavily coat the wires of a whisk. Remove pan from heat; add the salt and white pepper.

MARIO'S

TOMATO SAUCE

2 tablespoons olive oil
½ cup finely chopped onion
2 cups Italian plum or whole
    pack tomatoes, coarsely
    chopped, with juice
3 tablespoons tomato paste

1 tablespoon finely chopped
    fresh basil
1 teaspoon sugar
    Salt and freshly ground
    pepper

1. Heat the olive oil in a stainless steel saucepan. Add the onion; cook over moderate heat until soft but not brown.
2. Add the tomatoes, tomato paste, basil, sugar, salt, and a sprinkle of pepper. Reduce heat and simmer, partially covered, for approximately 45 minutes, stirring occasionally.
3. Press through a fine sieve into a bowl or pan. Season to taste. Serve hot.

INSALATA VERDE

3 ripe tomatoes
1 large head Boston lettuce,
    torn
3 anchovies, sliced
    lengthwise
4½ tablespoons red wine
    vinegar

1½ teaspoons crushed fresh
    basil
    Salt and pepper to taste
¾ cup olive oil

1. Cut each tomato into eight pieces. Arrange the lettuce, anchovy halves, and tomato slices attractively in individual bowls or plates.
2. Combine the vinegar, basil, and salt and white pepper in a small jar. Add the olive oil; cover and shake well. Adjust seasonings to taste.
3. Pour dressing over salad. Serve immediately.

LASAGNA VERDE PAVAROTTI

GREEN LASAGNA NOODLES	*Grated mozzarella cheese*
CHEESE SAUCE	*Grated Parmesan cheese*
MEAT SAUCE	*Butter*

1. Preheat oven to 375°.
2. Cover the bottom of a greased deep, round baking dish with one-third of the lasagna noodles. Cover with one-half the Cheese Sauce. Spread one-half the Meat Sauce over the Cheese Sauce. Repeat the layers, ending with a layer of noodles.
3. Sprinkle with the cheeses. Dot with butter. Bake in preheated oven 1 hour or until golden on top. Serve immediately.

GREEN LASAGNA NOODLES

Prepare and cook dough as directed in Green Pasta Dough recipe (see Cannelloni Signora Cristine) except roll out somewhat thicker than described and cut into 2-inch-wide strips.

CHEESE SAUCE

6 tablespoons butter	6 cups hot milk
6 tablespoons all-purpose flour	1 cup grated Parmesan cheese
1 teaspoon salt (approximately)	1 cup grated mozzarella cheese

1. Melt the butter in a heavy saucepan over moderate heat. Remove from heat; stir in the flour and salt. Cook, stirring constantly, until the flour dissolves. Do not let brown.
2. Gradually add the hot milk, stirring constantly with a wire whisk. Cook and stir until thickened and smooth.
3. Add the cheeses and stir until melted.

MARIO'S

MEAT SAUCE

6 tablespoons butter
3 tablespoons olive oil
1 onion, finely chopped
1 carrot, finely chopped
1 stalk celery, finely chopped
2 to 3 slices bacon, chopped
6 ounces minced pork
6 ounces minced beef
2 ounces sausage
3 chicken livers

1 cup dry white wine
Salt and pepper
2 tablespoons tomato paste
2 cups BEEF STOCK (see
   next page)
¼ pound mushrooms, chopped
½ clove garlic, pressed
½ cup chopped parsley
   (approximately)

1. Melt 3 tablespoons butter and the oil. Add the onion, carrot, celery, and bacon; fry gently until just beginning to brown.
2. Add the pork, beef, sausage, and liver. Add the wine and cook until it evaporates. Season with salt and pepper.
3. Dilute the tomato paste in the stock; add to the meat mixture. Cover and cook slowly for 1 hour.
4. Sauté the mushrooms, garlic, and chopped parsley in the remaining 3 tablespoons butter. Mix into the sauce.

MARIO'S

BEEF STOCK

2 pounds beef bones
2 medium-size carrots,
  coarsely chopped
½ stalk celery, coarsely
  chopped
1 onion, coarsely chopped

Pinch of thyme
8 peppercorns
1 bay leaf
3 ounces tomato paste
  (approximately)
1 clove garlic

1. Preheat oven to 350°. Bake the bones until browned, about 1 hour.
2. Place the bones in a large stock pot. Add the remaining ingredients and enough water to cover. Bring to a boil; boil about 2 hours.
3. Remove from heat and strain. Discard the bones and vegetables. Return the stock to the pot and cook over medium heat until reduced by one-half.

To make veal stock, simply substitute veal bones for the beef bones.

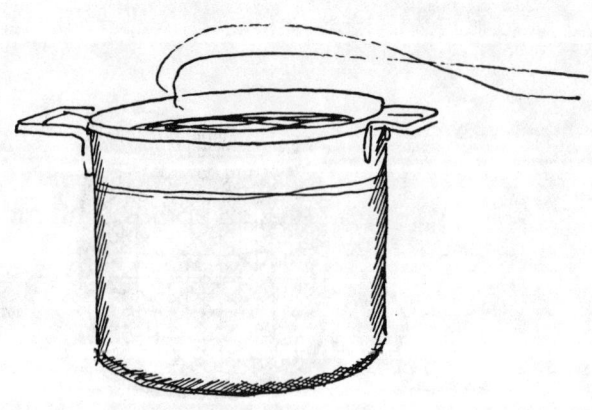

CANNOLI ALLA SICILIANA

1½ cups all-purpose flour
Pinch of salt
½ teaspoon baking powder
2 eggs
4 teaspoons sugar
2 tablespoons butter
1 cup Marsala or other red dessert wine (approximately)

Olive oil
½ pound ricotta cheese
4 teaspoons orange flower water
½ cup diced candied orange or citron
1 ounce bitter chocolate, crushed
Confectioners' sugar

1. Combine the flour, salt, baking powder, 1 egg, sugar, and butter; mix well.
2. Gradually add enough wine, a little at a time, to make a firm dough. Knead until smooth and elastic. Roll into very thin sheets; cut into twelve squares.
3. Place metal cannoli tubes diagonally onto each square so that the tube divides each square into two triangles. Lay the points of the triangles over the tubes so that they meet in the middle. Separate the remaining egg and use a little of the egg white to moisten the overlap. Press gently to seal.
4. Heat 3 to 4 inches olive oil in a deep pan. Fry the cannoli until golden brown, drain well on paper towels, and cool. Remove the metal tubes.
5. Combine the remaining part of the egg with the ricotta cheese, orange flower water, candied orange or citron, and chocolate and blend well. Fill cannoli with the cheese mixture. Sprinkle with confectioners' sugar.

The amount of wine needed to make a firm dough varies according to the flour used.

Serve two cannoli per serving.

Patry's

Dinner for Four

Crabmeat in Paprika Sauce

Caesar Salad with Patry's House Dressing

Chateaubriand

Caramel Custard

Wine:

Château Smith-Haut Lafitte

George Patry, Owner & Chef

Patry's is a pleasantly small French restaurant which is managed by Owner and Chef George Patry. Proprietor of a restaurant in his native France for thirty years, and later the first French chef at the Old Warsaw for ten years, he discovered through these experiences the secret to his restaurant's success: "We do our best to satisfy our customers."

One thing that never fails to satisfy is the cuisine. The menu consists of a limited selection of French dishes, each a specialty of George's, each impeccably prepared. While he is busy in the kitchen, his wife and daughter greet guests at the door. Over its fourteen years of business, Patry's has secured a very loyal clientele; even the conventioneers are regulars. Most diners are known by name, and if the kitchen staff were able to see them enter, they could probably begin to prepare the guests' meals before they were even ordered.

A patron can count on consistently good quality at Patry's, for the only individual sharing cooking responsibilities with the owner/chef was trained by a very able person, George Patry himself.

2504 McKinney Avenue

CRABMEAT IN PAPRIKA SAUCE

2 tablespoons finely
   chopped shallots
6 tablespoons butter
1 cup dry white wine
2 teaspoons Spanish paprika
2 tablespoons all-purpose
   flour

2 cups milk
¼ cup whipping cream
¾ pound Alaskan king crab
4 to 8 fresh mushrooms, sliced
   Chopped parsley

1. Preheat oven to 400°.
2. Sauté the shallots in 2 tablespoons butter until golden brown. Stir in the wine and paprika; slowly bring to a boil. Remove from heat and set aside.
3. Melt the remaining 4 tablespoons butter in a saucepan. Stir in the flour; cook, stirring constantly, for 5 minutes.
4. Add the milk. Cook and stir until smooth and thickened. Stir in the shallot mixture and bring to a boil.
5. Add the whipping cream gradually, stirring constantly. As soon as the cream is incorporated, remove from heat.
6. Place 3 ounces crabmeat in each of four individual casseroles or scallop shells. Divide the mushrooms equally among the dishes. Pour the sauce over.
7. Bake in preheated oven for 5 to 7 minutes. Garnish with chopped parsley.

The sautéed shallots should be the color of hazelnuts when done.

The crab may be served in an au gratin dish instead of individual dishes.

The sauce may be stored in a refrigerator for up to one week. It is good with other seafoods, too.

CAESAR SALAD

2 *level teaspoons minced garlic*

2 *heaping teaspoons dry mustard*

6 *anchovies*

1 *teaspoon Worcestershire sauce*

2 *egg yolks*

PATRY'S HOUSE DRESSING

2 *heads romaine lettuce, cut into thirds*

1 *cup croutons*

½ *cup grated Parmesan cheese*

Salt and pepper to taste

1. Combine the garlic, mustard, anchovies, and Worcestershire sauce in a large wooden bowl. Mash against sides of the bowl until a thick paste is formed.
2. Blend in the egg yolks. Add the dressing, romaine, croutons, and cheese; toss well.
3. Add salt and pepper to taste. Serve on chilled plates.

PATRY'S HOUSE DRESSING

1 tablespoon Dijon-style
  mustard
⅓ cup red wine vinegar

1⅓ cups vegetable oil
Salt and pepper to taste

Combine the mustard and vinegar, mixing well. Slowly add the oil, beating constantly, until the dressing begins to thicken. Season to taste.

For the dressing to thicken, mustard and vinegar must be mixed together before the oil is added.

CHATEAUBRIAND

¼ cup chopped shallots
4 tablespoons butter, melted
2 teaspoons finely ground
   black pepper
2¼ cups burgundy

2 cups Brown Sauce
   (see index)
¼ cup cornstarch
2 (24-ounce) center cuts
   beef tenderloin

1. Sauté the shallots in the butter until golden. Add the pepper and 2 cups of the wine; bring to a boil. Stir in the brown sauce and return to a boil.

2. Combine the cornstarch and 3 to 4 tablespoons wine to form a paste; add to the wine sauce. Cook, stirring constantly, until thickened, about 10 to 15 minutes.

3. Pound the tenderloin to 2½ inches thick. Grill or broil to rare or medium-rare.

4. Tear off a 30-inch piece of extra-heavy duty aluminum foil. Fold in half. Cut into the shape of a circle. Fold the edges over, leaving an opening of several inches. Pound the folds with the flat of a heavy knife to seal. Fold over and pound to seal once more.

5. Place the meat in the foil pouch. Pour in the sauce; seal the pouch with a double fold. Place a large, oiled, heat-proof platter over medium heat. Place the pouch on the platter and cook about 2 minutes, or until the pouch puffs up. Remove the platter from heat.

6. Slit the top of the pouch. Transfer the meat to a cutting board and slice ½ inch thick. Serve with the sauce from the pouch.

You will smell a wonderful aroma when you slit the pouch open.

CARAMEL CUSTARD

¾ cup sugar
3 eggs, beaten

1 teaspoon vanilla extract
2 cups milk, scalded

1. Preheat oven to 400°.
2. Combine ¼ cup of the sugar with ⅓ cup water in a large saucepan or a skillet. Cook over very low heat, stirring constantly, until the sugar melts and is a light brown color. Pour into four custard cups and set aside.
3. Combine the eggs, remaining ½ cup sugar, and vanilla in a saucepan; mix well.
4. Gradually add the milk, stirring rapidly and constantly with a wire whisk until thoroughly blended. Pour the custard mixture over the browned sugar, filling almost to the top of the cups. Place the cups in a large baking pan. Fill the pan with hot water to half-way up the sides of the custard cups.
7. Bake in preheated oven for 45 minutes or until the custard is firm and lightly browned. Cool to room temperature; refrigerate until serving.

PLUM BLOSSOM

Dinner for Eight

Winter Melon Soup
or
Chicken Cream Soup

Lobster Rolls

Barbecued Spareribs

Shrimp Toast

Red Shrimp and White Baby Shrimp

Beef and Broccoli

Sea Scallops with Oyster Sauce

Almond-Fried Ice Cream

Wine:
Wang Fu

Randy L. Gantenbin, Executive Director, Food and Beverage
Hector Chang, Chef

*T*he Plum Blossom, located on the western side of Atrium II in Loew's Anatole-Dallas, provides a leisurely, subdued dining atmosphere with authentic cuisine from several regions of China. The decor, as serene as the name, features the celadon green and rich plum colors most often found in artifacts of ancient China. The dining area, centering around a seven-foot bronze Buddha, several large scrolls, and a black lacquered console with mother-of-pearl inlay, gives guests a feeling of dining in Imperial Chinese style. Even the exquisite table settings have been imported from China.

Chef Hector Chang supervises the staff. A full menu of à la carte delicacies features a variety of regional dishes, complemented by wines imported from China. The most extensive of the three multi-course banquet combinations is "The Great Imperial Banquet," which features: a ten-flavor chrysanthemum firepot with seafoods, chicken, beef, oysters, vegetables, and noodles; winter melon soup; traditional Peking duck pancakes; large red shrimp in-shell and white baby shrimp; heart of Chinese cabbage; sweet and sour pork, Lichee-style; lichee fruit stuffed with cream cheese and candied yue-sai; almond fried ice cream and tangerine sauce; and a selection of rare Chinese teas.

Loew's Anatole-Dallas
2201 Stemmons Freeway North

WINTER MELON SOUP

1 gallon Chicken Stock (see index)
¼ pound dried black mushrooms, diced
3 ounces chicken meat, diced
3 ounces fresh pork, diced
1 pound winter melon, diced
3 ounces shrimp, diced
Salt and pepper to taste

1. Heat the chicken stock to boiling; add the black mushrooms and cook 5 minutes.
2. Add the chicken and pork; cook an additional 5 minutes.
3. Add the melon and shrimp. Cook until the melon is tender.
4. Add salt and pepper to taste and serve while hot.

CHICKEN CREAM SOUP

2 quarts Chicken Stock (see index)
1½ pounds creamed corn
½ pound fresh chicken meat, diced
6 tablespoons cornstarch
4 egg whites
2 teaspoons salt
2 tablespoons sugar
1 teaspoon white pepper

1. Heat the chicken stock to boiling; add the corn and cook 5 minutes.
2. Place the chicken in a bowl. Sprinkle with 2 tablespoons cornstarch and add 2 egg whites. Stir together 1 minute.
3. Sauté the chicken in a lightly oiled skillet over medium heat for about 2 minutes; remove and reserve.
4. Dissolve the remaining cornstarch in ¾ cup cool water; add the salt, sugar, pepper, and the dissolved cornstarch into the hot soup. Stir until thick and smooth.
5. Beat the remaining 2 egg whites and add with the cooked chicken to the soup. Heat almost to a boil and serve.

LOBSTER ROLLS

1 pound lobster meat,
  diced
¼ cup bamboo shoots,
  finely chopped
¼ cup water chestnuts,
  finely chopped

½ teaspoon garlic powder
½ teaspoon salt
8 eggroll skins
2 tablespoons flour
  Oil for deep-frying

1. Combine the lobster, bamboo shoots, water chestnuts, and seasonings.
2. Place some of the mixture near one edge of each of the eggroll skins. Begin rolling, jelly roll fashion; after the first turn, fold the ends toward the center and continue rolling.
3. Mix the flour with enough cold water to form a paste in a small bowl. Seal the edges of the lobster rolls with the paste.
4. Heat the oil until almost smoking in a wok or deep pan. When hot, deep-fry the rolls until golden brown, about 2 to 3 minutes. Drain and serve while hot.

BARBECUED SPARERIBS

3 pounds pork spareribs
1 cup sugar

1 tablespoon salt
  BARBECUE SAUCE

1. Place the ribs on a counter and remove the covering skin. Sprinkle with the sugar and salt and rub in well; let rest 30 minutes.
2. Brush the Barbecue Sauce over the ribs and set aside another 30 minutes.
3. Cook in a covered charcoal grill or a 375° oven for 45 minutes to 1 hour. Cut the ribs apart and serve.

BARBECUE SAUCE

2 cups hoisin sauce	2 tablespoons vinegar
1½ cups sugar	1 teaspoon five spice powder
¼ cup honey	½ cup tomato catsup
¼ cup soy sauce	2 tablespoons salt

Combine all ingredients. Use as a basting sauce for spareribs.

SHRIMP TOAST

1 pound shrimp, peeled and deveined	5 tablespoons cornstarch
¼ pound water chestnuts	Salt and white pepper to taste
½ cup chopped fresh cilantro	8 slices white bread
¼ pound fresh pork fat	½ cup white sesame seeds
4 egg whites	Oil for deep-frying

1. Chop the shrimp, water chestnuts, and cilantro very fine.
2. Grind the pork fat and add to the shrimp mixture.
3. Stir the egg whites one at a time into the mixture. Add the cornstarch and stir with a wooden spoon for several minutes until very thick. Season with salt and white pepper.
4. Remove the crusts from the bread. Cut each slice in half.
5. Spread the bread halves with the shrimp mixture and sprinkle the surface with sesame seeds.
6. Deep-fry in hot cooking oil until golden. Drain on paper towels, arrange on a platter, and serve while hot.

Cilantro is sometimes found under the names Chinese parsley or fresh coriander.

RED SHRIMP AND WHITE BABY SHRIMP

*2 tablespoons plus 2
  teaspoons cornstarch*
2 egg whites
*½ pound small cocktail
  shrimp*
½ cup cooking oil

*1 pound large fresh shrimp,
  peeled and deveined*
2 tablespoons sherry
*⅓ cup Chicken Stock
  (see index)*
Salt and pepper to taste

1. Mix together 2 tablespoons cornstarch and the egg whites. Add the baby shrimp and stir to coat well; marinate 5 minutes.
2. Heat a wok or skillet and add the cooking oil. When the oil is hot, fry the large shrimp for 2 minutes, stirring constantly.
3. Add the sherry, stir quickly, and remove the shrimp to a serving platter with a slotted spoon.
4. Immediately add the coated baby shrimp to the wok and stir quickly until heated. Add the chicken stock and season to taste with salt and pepper.
5. Dissolve the remaining cornstarch in 1 tablespoon cool water and stir into the wok mixture to form a thick sauce. Empty the contents of the wok onto the serving platter beside the large shrimp. Serve while hot.

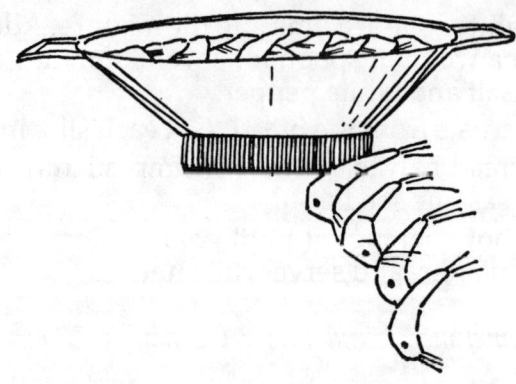

BEEF AND BROCCOLI

1 teaspoon garlic powder	1 bunch broccoli
1 teaspoon salt	¾ cup cooking oil
2 tablespoons plus 2 teaspoons cornstarch	⅔ cup Chicken Stock (see index)
2 eggs	2 tablespoons soy sauce
1 pound beef tenderloin, cut into 1½" cubes	2 dashes Tabasco sauce

1. Make a mixture of the garlic powder, salt, 2 tablespoons cornstarch, and eggs. Stir in the beef, coating thoroughly. Marinate 5 minutes.
2. Separate the broccoli into florets, leaving sections of stalk attached. Cook 3 minutes in lightly salted boiling water. Remove and keep hot.
3. Heat a wok or skillet and add the cooking oil. When oil is hot, cook the beef about 1 minute, or until browned, stirring constantly.
4. Drain off the cooking oil. Add chicken stock, soy sauce, and Tabasco sauce and return to heat.
5. Dissolve the remaining cornstarch in 1 tablespoon cold water and stir into the beef mixture to form a sauce.
6. Immediately place the beef in the center of a serving platter and surround with broccoli. Serve hot.

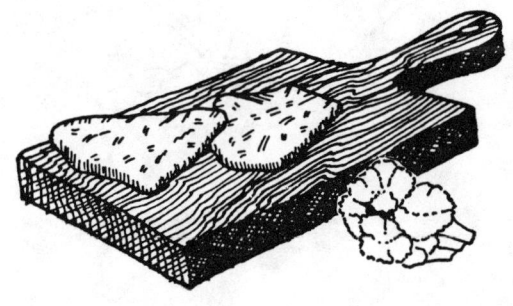

SEA SCALLOPS WITH OYSTER SAUCE

¼ *pound straw mushrooms*
¾ *cup Chicken Stock*
   (see index)
¼ *cup sherry*
 2 *teaspoons cornstarch*

3 *tablespoons cooking oil*
½ *pound sea scallops*
3 *ounces oyster sauce*
1 *teaspoon sugar*
½ *teaspoon salt*

1. Simmer the mushrooms in the chicken stock and wine for 5 minutes. Drain and reserve the broth and mushrooms separately.
2. Dissolve the cornstarch in 1 tablespoon cool water and set aside.
3. Heat a wok or skillet and add the oil. When hot, add the scallops, stir-frying 1 minute.
4. Add the reserved mushrooms and cook 30 seconds.
5. Add the reserved chicken stock, oyster sauce, sugar, and salt; stir well.
6. Add the dissolved cornstarch and stir while the sauce thickens. Empty the contents to a platter and serve while hot.

ALMOND-FRIED ICE CREAM

8 scoops vanilla ice cream	1 cup tangerine sauce
Oil for deep-frying	2 cups sliced almonds

1. Scoop the ice cream in advance; return to freezer until extremely hard.
2. Heat the cooking oil in a deep-fryer.
3. Roll each ice-cream ball in the tangerine sauce, then in the sliced almonds, coating thoroughly.
4. Deep-fry for a few seconds only. Serve immediately.

Dinner for Four

Avocado Princess

Mateus Sorbet

Veal Gourmet

Soufflées Potatoes

Pyramid Salad

Soufflé Grand Marnier

Glazed Strawberries

Wine:

Chablis or Bordeaux

Heinz Muller, Food and Beverage Director

Bernard Malfait, Executive Chef

*T*he Pyramid Room in the elegant Fairmont Hotel has been since its inception
the epitome of fine dining in Dallas. Its elaborate dining room
and extensive menu combine to give the restaurant a well-
earned and outstanding reputation.

The behind-the-scenes creative genius of the Pyramid
Room is Executive Chef Bernard Malfait. Trained in the best
restaurants around his native Nancy, France, he also lived in
Canada before moving further south. "Coming to America
was a dream come true for me," he said. "I loved Texas from
the moment I arrived here, and it has been home for me ever
since." His first job at the Pyramid Room was one of cook.
After five years he left the hotel's kitchens to open his own restaurant, but the opportunity to possibly become executive
chef lured him back one year later. As he proudly notes, "This
is the kind of position almost every chef covets the most—a
prestigious job with an internationally known hotel."

Coupled with the skill of the other employees of the
Pyramid Room, his expertise has helped win for the hotel
numerous awards for culinary excellence. By any standards
and by all critical reviews, the Pyramid Room is an excellent
restaurant which consistently offers the best fine dining.

Fairmont Hotel
Ross at Akard

AVOCADO PRINCESS

2 tablespoons diced onion
¼ pound plus 2 tablespoons
  butter, melted
¼ pound bay shrimp, finely
  diced
¼ pound crabmeat, finely
  diced
12 fresh mushrooms, finely
  diced
2 teaspoons paprika
6 tablespoons all-purpose
  flour

¼ cup brandy
1 cup whipping cream
  Salt and pepper to taste
2 avocados, peeled and
  halved
4 eggs, poached
  CHEESE SAUCE (see
  next page)
¼ cup grated Parmesan
  cheese

1. Preheat oven to 300°.
2. Sauté the onion in ¼ pound butter. Add the shrimp, crab, and mushrooms; sauté 5 minutes.
3. Stir in the paprika and flour. Cook, stirring constantly, for 2 minutes.
4. Add the brandy, cream, and salt and pepper. Cook over low heat 10 minutes. Remove from heat; set aside and keep warm.
5. Arrange the avocado halves on a serving tray. Place a small amount of the remaining butter in the cavity of each half. Spoon the seafood mixture into the avocados. Top each with a poached egg. Spoon the Cheese Sauce over the eggs.
6. Sprinkle with Parmesan cheese. Bake in preheated oven for 10 minutes.

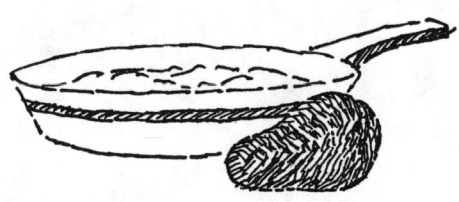

CHEESE SAUCE

¼ pound butter, melted
2 tablespoons all-purpose
  flour
2 cups milk

Salt and pepper to taste
Dash of nutmeg
½ cup grated Parmesan
  cheese

1. Blend the butter and flour in a saucepan; cook, stirring constantly, for 5 minutes.
2. Stir in the milk. Cook 15 minutes, stirring constantly, until smooth and thickened.
3. Stir in the salt, pepper, and nutmeg. Just before using, stir in the cheese.

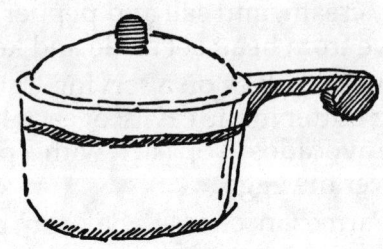

MATEUS SORBET

1 *cup sugar*
1¾ *cups Mateus rosé wine*

FROSTED GRAPES

1. Combine 2¾ cups water and the sugar in a saucepan; bring to a boil and cook 5 minutes. Remove from heat.
2. Stir in the wine. Allow to cool.
3. Pour into a 1½-quart rectangular pan; freeze.
4. To serve, scrape the frozen sorbet into flakes and spoon into chilled or frozen glasses. Serve with Frosted Grapes.

FROSTED GRAPES

½ *pound grapes*
4 *egg whites*

Sugar

1. Break the grapes into four clusters; set aside.
2. Beat the egg whites and 1 cup water until frothy.
3. Dip the grape clusters into the egg white mixture and roll in the sugar. Set aside to dry on waxed paper.

VEAL GOURMET

½ cup diced celery
½ cup plus 1 tablespoon
   butter
8 (3-ounce) veal loin cutlets
8 slices Swiss cheese
4 slices prosciutto ham
   Salt and pepper

½ cup all-purpose flour
2 apples, peeled and cut
   into eighths
2 cups whipping cream
½ cup Beef Stock (see index)
   or veal stock
BÉARNAISE SAUCE

1. Sauté the celery in 1 tablespoon butter until tender; set aside to cool.
2. Lightly pound the veal on both sides. Layer 1 slice cheese, ham, and another slice cheese on each of four cutlets. Top each with another cutlet; secure with toothpicks.
3. Sprinkle with salt and pepper and dredge in flour. Sauté in 6 tablespoons butter for 10 minutes on each side. Remove from pan.
4. Sprinkle the reserved celery on a serving platter; top with the veal. Keep warm.
5. Sauté the apples in the remaining 2 tablespoons butter about 2 minutes.
6. Add the cream and stock, stirring constantly. Cook until thickened. Correct the seasonings to taste and pour the sauce over the cutlets.
7. Top each cutlet with some of the Béarnaise Sauce. Broil just until glazed, watching carefully. Pour the remaining Béarnaise Sauce around the cutlets and serve at once.

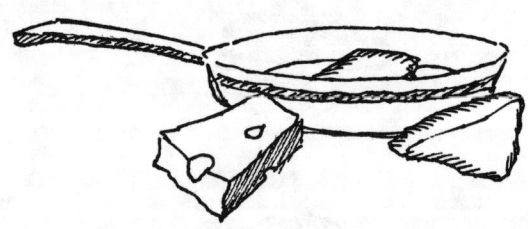

PYRAMID ROOM

BÉARNAISE SAUCE

4 egg yolks
½ pound plus 2 tablespoons
butter, melted
Salt and pepper

Juice of 1 lemon
1 medium shallot, chopped
2 tablespoons tarragon
2 tablespoons vinegar

1. Beat the egg yolks very well. Place in the top of a double boiler and cook over medium heat for 3 minutes, stirring constantly and vigorously. Remove from heat.
2. Add the butter very slowly, stirring constantly.
3. Stir in the salt, pepper, and lemon juice. Add the remaining ingredients and stir to mix.

Have the egg yolks and butter at the same temperature before making the Béarnaise Sauce. And be sure to use butter—not margarine.

SOUFFLÉES POTATOES

6 large potatoes   *Salt and pepper*
1 gallon cooking oil

1. Peel the potatoes. Trim the sides and ends to form into rectangular blocks. Slice into very thin strips, about ⅒ inch thick. Place the strips in water to cover as they are sliced.
2. Fill two deep-fryers with 2 quarts oil each. Heat the first fryer to 280° and the second to 350°.
3. Remove the potatoes from the water and wipe dry with a cloth. Drop the strips, one at a time, into the 280° fryer. Shake the fryer basket constantly to keep the potatoes from sticking together. Cook until the potatoes begin to puff out.
4. Remove the strips from the first fryer and drain; immediately drop into the second fryer. Cook, shaking the fryer basket constantly, until the potatoes are well-parched. Remove and drain on a cloth.
5. Place the potatoes in a single layer on a baking sheet and refrigerate until serving time. Just before serving, plunge into hot deep oil until very puffed and dry. Remove with a strainer. Sprinkle with salt and pepper. Serve on absorbent cloth or decorative paper.

Note: If preparing at least a day ahead, follow this recipe through step 4. Place the blanched potatoes on a baking sheet and freeze until solid. Transfer to a freezer bag and store in the freezer until needed. When ready to use, thaw 30 minutes at room temperature and proceed as in step 5.

PYRAMID SALAD

2 heads Boston lettuce	4 ripe olives
1 head Belgian endive	4 artichoke hearts
1 small bunch watercress, cleaned	*PYRAMID SALAD DRESSING*
8 cherry tomatoes	

1. Core the lettuce and break the leaves apart, retaining the hearts whole. Tear the leaves into bite-size pieces. Break the endive into separate leaves. Wash both and dry well.
2. Arrange the lettuce on four individual salad plates, with a lettuce heart in the center of each. Arrange the endive leaves over, radiating out from the center into a star pattern.
3. Make a small mound of watercress in the center of each salad. Garnish with 2 tomatoes, 1 olive, and 1 artichoke heart apiece. Serve with Pyramid Salad Dressing.

PYRAMID SALAD DRESSING

2 egg yolks	*Salt and pepper*
¼ cup red wine vinegar	1 cup corn oil
2 tablespoons Dijon mustard	

1. Combine the egg yolks, vinegar, mustard, and salt and pepper in a mixing bowl; mix well.
2. Slowly add the oil, about a tablespoon at a time, beating constantly with a rotary or electric beater.
3. Stir in enough warm water to thin. The consistency should be thinner than mayonnaise.

SOUFFLÉ GRAND MARNIER

3 egg yolks	4 egg whites
¼ cup sugar	⅛ teaspoon cream of tartar
¼ cup Grand Marnier liqueur	Powdered sugar
1½ teaspoons grated orange peel	VANILLA SAUCE

1. Preheat oven to 425°. Butter the bottom and sides of a 1½-quart ovenproof soufflé dish. Dust with sugar, shaking the dish to coat the bottom and sides well. Discard any excess sugar. Set the dish aside.

2. Beat the egg yolks well in the top of a double boiler. Slowly add the sugar, beating until the yolks are very thick and pale yellow.

3. Set the pan over barely simmering—not boiling—water. Cook, stirring constantly with a wooden spoon or rubber spatula, until the mixture thickens.

4. Stir in the liqueur and orange peel. Pour the mixture into a large bowl. Place the bowl in a larger pan filled with crushed ice and cold water. Stir until cold. Remove the bowl from the ice and set aside.

5. Beat the egg whites in a large bowl until foamy. Add the cream of tartar and beat until stiff peaks form.

6. Fold a large spoonful of the beaten egg whites into the yolk mixture with a rubber spatula. Fold in the remaining whites. Spoon the mixture into the prepared soufflé dish, filling to within 2 inches of the top.

7. Smooth the top with a spatula. For a decorative effect, cut a trench 1 inch deep around the top, about 1 inch from the edge. Bake on the middle shelf of preheated oven for 2 minutes. Reduce heat to 400° and bake 20 to 30 minutes, or until the soufflé has risen about 2 inches above the top of the dish and the top is lightly browned.

8. Sprinkle with powdered sugar. Puncture the soufflé in the center; pour Vanilla Sauce over.

VANILLA SAUCE

2 cups milk	6 tablespoons sugar
4 egg yolks	2 tablespoons vanilla extract

1. Bring the milk to a boil.
2. Beat the egg yolks, sugar, and vanilla together well.
3. Pour the milk quickly over the egg mixture, stirring briskly to keep the eggs from cooking.
4. Set the dish in cold water immediately to stop the cooking. Cool.
5. Warm the sauce slightly before serving. Adjust seasoning to taste, adding more vanilla if desired.

An unlined copper bowl is ideal for beating egg whites.

GLAZED STRAWBERRIES

8 large strawberries	2 tablespoons corn syrup
1 cup plus 2 tablespoons sugar	

1 Wash the strawberries; do not remove stems and caps. Drain on a cloth until dry.
2. Lightly oil a baking sheet. Sprinkle with 2 tablespoons sugar and set aside.
3 Combine the remaining sugar, 1 cup water, and the corn syrup in a saucepan. Mix well. Cook to 350° on a candy thermometer. Remove from heat and place the pan in cold water for at least 5 seconds.
4. Holding by the stem, dip each berry in the sugar mixture. Place on the prepared pan. Cool 5 minutes; serve within 1 hour.

It is essential to use a candy thermometer for accuracy.

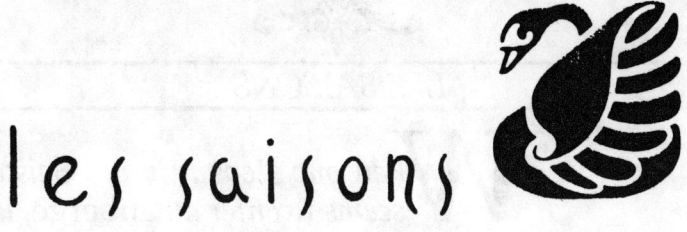

les saisons

Dinner for Four

Potage de Cresson

Escalopes de Veau Normande

Pommes de Terre au Gratin

Tarte aux Poires

Wine:

Chablis Grand Cru, Les Clos, Simon

Phil Vaccaro, Owner

Jean LaFont, Executive Chef

Daniel Roger, Chef de Cuisine

*W*hen one steps into Les Saisons, he seems to enter an auberge, an out-of-town restaurant where the French retreat to relax and enjoy good food. Decorated in pastel colors, it is accented with paintings, large wall murals, and tile walls that were actually taken from a French spa of the early twentieth century, so that the ambiance is one of a beautiful French country restaurant. One tends not to forget his location, however, because in the midst of these unusual surroundings he can look out onto a spectacular view of the Dallas skyline.

In addition to the regular and outstanding cuisine, Les Saisons offers a special menu on alternate weeks which features an appetizer, entrée, and dessert from a province in France. At lunchtime, the quiet and beauty of the restaurant makes it conducive to business tête-à-têtes. At dinner, the candlelit glow and live harp music makes it an ideal choice for a romantic dinner.

165 Turtle Creek Village

POTAGE DE CRESSON

2 tablespoons butter
1 onion, minced
2 bunches watercress,
   washed, dried, and
   chopped
2 medium-size potatoes,
   peeled and diced

2 pinches of salt
Pinch of white pepper
½ teaspoon sugar
½ cup whipping cream, at
   room temperature

1. Melt the butter in a large saucepan. Add the onion and sauté over medium-high heat until soft.
2. Set aside ½ cup watercress leaves for garnish. Add the remaining watercress, the potatoes, salt, white pepper, sugar, and 4 cups water to the saucepan. Simmer 25 minutes.
3. Pour the soup into an electric blender and purée until smooth. Pour into a serving dish; stir in the cream and reserved watercress leaves. Adjust the seasonings to taste.

Watercress has a special taste of its own—slightly bitter and piquant— which recalls the taste of mustard. Carefully pick it over before using, removing any yellow leaves and the thicker stems. Wash quickly in running water and never let it soak.

ESCALOPES DE VEAU NORMANDE

2 pounds veal (preferably
   loin or bottom round)
Salt and pepper
½ cup all-purpose flour
3 tablespoons butter
1 tablespoon vegetable oil

2 large apples, peeled,
   cored, and cut into
   eighths
1 ounce Calvados
2 cups plus 2 tablespoons
   whipping cream

1. Slice the veal into ¼-inch slices; place between two sheets of waxed paper and pound to ⅛-inch thickness. Sprinkle with salt and pepper and dredge in the flour.
2. Melt 1 tablespoon butter and the oil in a skillet over medium heat. Add the veal and sauté. When done, place the veal in a serving dish, set aside, and keep warm.
3. Sauté the apples in the remaining butter until soft. Pour the Calvados over the apples and add the whipping cream; simmer until thickened.
4. Preheat the broiler.
5. When the apples are done, spoon over the veal scallops and pour the sauce over the apples. Broil for 30 seconds or until nicely glazed.

POMMES DE TERRE AU GRATIN

2 pounds potatoes, peeled
   and minced
Salt and white pepper
½ cup grated Swiss cheese

2 cups whipping cream
4 eggs, beaten
Pinch of nutmeg

1. Preheat oven to 375°.
2. Sprinkle the potatoes lightly with salt and white pepper. Layer the potatoes and cheese in a buttered baking dish.
3. Mix together the cream, eggs, and nutmeg. Pour over the potatoes. Sprinkle with salt and pepper to taste. Bake in preheated oven 70 minutes. When done, serve immediately.

TARTE AUX POIRES

2¾ cups sugar
1 vanilla bean
12 pears, peeled, halved,
   and cored
   PÂTE BRISÉE
½ pound almond powder

4 eggs, lightly beaten
4 tablespoons sweet butter,
   softened
1 drop of almond extract
   MERINGUE

1. Combine 2 cups sugar and the vanilla bean with 10 cups water in a large saucepan; bring to a boil. Cook until the sugar dissolves.
2. Add the pears to the syrup and simmer until tender. Strain, pat dry, slice, and set aside.
3. Roll out the Pâte Brisée to fit a 10 or 12-inch tart pan; place in the pan. Preheat oven to 350°.
4. Combine the almond powder, ¾ cup sugar, the eggs, butter, and almond extract and mix well. Spread the mixture in the tart shell. Arrange the pear slices in a circular pattern on top with the slices facing toward the center of the tart. Bake in preheated oven 35 minutes.
5. While the tart is baking, prepare the Meringue and place in a pastry bag.
6. When the tart is done, remove from oven and increase the temperature to 450°. Pipe Meringue on top of each pear slice. Bake for 4 minutes more; serve at once.

PÂTE BRISÉE

½ pound butter, softened
1 egg yolk, lightly beaten

2 cups all-purpose flour
   Pinch of salt

Combine the butter, egg yolk, and ½ cup water; blend well. Add the flour and salt and mix well. Chill 2 hours before using.

MERINGUE

4 egg whites, at room
   temperature

1 drop of vanilla extract
1 cup sugar

Combine the egg whites and vanilla; beat until foamy. Very gradually add the sugar, beating until stiff.

Dinner for Four

Scampi Giovanni

Tagliarini Verdi Gratinati al Prosciutto

Insalata Verde

Costate di Vitello Fantasia

Carote alla Marsala

Royal Danieli

Wine:
Pinto Grígio dell' Alto Adige
or
Orvieto Secco

Mario A. Messina, Proprietor
Sam Machi, Master Chef

Il Sorrento is a restaurant whose interior architecture is as magical and special as its cuisine. Through façades and reliefs, a trompe l'oeil effect gives one the impression of being in Old World Italy. Picturesque buildings with tiled roofs surround a life-size statue of a Roman hero. Grapevines wind up the seemingly real columned porches, and images of pigeons on the roof add to the illusion. The dining tables, which are visited by strolling musicians, are arranged so as to give the appearance of forming a town square. To complete the charming effect, a real waterway runs through the restaurant, and on it a gondola rides as if on a canal.

When it originally opened in 1952 at another location, Il Sorrento was a small restaurant which sat just fifty-five individuals. The original menu was limited as well, offering largely the basics of Italian cuisine: spaghetti, meatballs, and veal dishes. As the restaurant expanded, so did the tastes of the customers, and owner Mario A. Messini began presenting more specialty dishes, so that the menu is now rather extensive. Mario is always present to greet his guests, but just as frequently can be seen slipping an apron over his suit in order to assist Chef Sam Machi. If one desires not only sumptuous Italian dining, but also the ambiance of another world, Il Sorrento can more than satisfy.

8616 Turtle Creek Boulevard at Northwest Highway

SCAMPI GIOVANNI

¼ pound butter
4 large cloves garlic, finely
  chopped
1 tablespoon chopped parsley
  Pinch of oregano
  Salt and pepper to taste

1 pound Danish lobster
  tails, shelled
  Seasoned bread crumbs
  Juice of 1 lemon
  Lemon wedges

1. Preheat oven to 400°.
2. In a blender, make a paste of the butter, garlic, parsley, and seasonings.
3. Butterfly the lobster tails, leaving the tips intact.
4. Place a generous amount of the butter mixture on each tail. Coat with bread crumbs and place in a baking pan. Bake in preheated oven 10 minutes.
5. Place the lobster tails on a serving platter. Squeeze the lemon juice into the butter sauce in the baking pan; agitate and pour over the lobster. Garnish with lemon wedges and serve.

Shrimp may be substituted for the Danish lobster tails—use 10 to 15-count shrimp.

TAGLIARINI VERDI GRATINATA AL PROSCIUTTO
Baked Green Noodles with Prosciutto

½ pound narrow green
   noodles
4 tablespoons butter
3 ounces prosciutto ham,
   coarsely chopped

1 cup heavy cream
3 ounces Parmesan cheese,
   grated
4 slices mozzarella cheese
1 cup TOMATO SAUCE

1. Boil the green noodles in salted water until al dente. Drain and toss in the butter.
2. Preheat oven to 400°.
3. Place the noodles in a casserole and sprinkle with the chopped prosciutto.
4. Combine the cream with the Parmesan and pour over the noodles.
5. Top with slices of mozzarella.
6. Spread Tomato Sauce over all and bake in preheated oven until bubbly. Serve hot in the casserole.

TOMATO SAUCE

1 cup drained tomatoes
6 tablespoons butter

Salt and pepper
Pinch of nutmeg

1. Chop the tomatoes very fine.
2. Cook in butter with salt, pepper, and nutmeg until the liquid evaporates.

INSALATA VERDE
Green Salad

1 small head lettuce	½ teaspoon celery salt
½ bunch watercress	Pinch of coarsely ground
Few leaves of endive	black pepper
1 tablespoon wine vinegar	1 whole tomato, quartered
¼ cup salad oil	

1. Wash, drain, and crisp the greens.
2. Combine the vinegar, oil, celery salt, and pepper.
3. Add dressing to greens and mix well.
4. Mound on four individual salad plates, garnishing each with a to-mato wedge.

COSTATE DI VITELLO FANTASIA
Veal Chops Fantasia

4 veal rib chops
Salt and pepper
3 to 4 tablespoons clarified
butter
3 ounces mushrooms,
thinly sliced
Butter
DUCHESS POTATOES
1 small tomato, peeled
and sliced

¼ pound liver pâté
1 cup Béchamel Sauce (see
index), mixed with
1 teaspoon tomato paste
2 to 4 tablespoons grated
Parmesan cheese
Watercress leaves

1. Flatten the veal chops and score the edges. Sprinkle with salt and pepper.
2. Brown the chops lightly on one side in the clarified butter.
3. Lay the chops cooked side up on a buttered baking sheet. Preheat oven to 400°.
4. Sauté the mushrooms in the butter.
5. Pipe a border of Duchess Potatoes around the edge of each chop. Fill the centers with the sautéed mushrooms.
6. Cover the mushrooms with 1 slice tomato per chop. Top with liver pâté.
7. Cover each portion of pâté with Béchamel Sauce and sprinkle with Parmesan. Bake in preheated oven until cheese browns.
8. Arrange the veal chops on a platter. Garnish with watercress and serve.

DUCHESS POTATOES

6 medium-size mature
potatoes
1 egg
2 egg yolks
2 tablespoons butter

¾ teaspoon salt
Pinch of pepper
Freshly grated nutmeg
to taste
1 to 2 tablespoons milk (optional)

1. Wash and pare the potatoes, removing any blemishes. Quarter and place in cold salted water to cover. Bring just to a boil. Reduce heat and simmer about 20 minutes, or until fork-tender but not mushy.
2. Drain well and put through a sieve or ricer to obtain an even consistency.
3. Beat the egg and yolks together. Add the eggs, butter, and seasonings to the potatoes, beating constantly with a wooden spoon until fluffy and absolutely without lumps. A tablespoon or two of milk can be added at this time if the potatoes seem too firm for a pastry bag. Set aside to cool slightly.
4. Fill pastry tube with the still-warm potatoes and pipe as recipe indicates.

Potatoes brought to a boil from a cold-water start cook more evenly and have less tendency to break up or become mushy.

Costate di Vitello Fantasia is an exciting presentation and can be easily prepared long before serving. It is one of my favorites for banquet parties or small groups.

CAROTE ALLA MARSALA
Carrots with Marsala Wine

1 pound carrots, peeled	Salt and white pepper
4 to 6 tablespoons butter	to taste
3 to 4 ounces Marsala or Madeira	Parsley sprigs (optional)

1. Boil the carrots in salted water until tender. Remove from water.
2. Place the carrots, butter, wine, and salt and pepper in a food processor or blender and blend until puréed.
3. Serve in a casserole, garnished with parsley sprigs if desired.

This is one of our favorite preparations of vegetables—it's unique, and it lends great color to a dish. It usually creates favorable comments and many requests for extra servings.

ROYAL DANIELI

½ cup fruit cocktail	Whipped cream
½ cup maraschino liqueur	SPUN SUGAR YARN
4 scoops vanilla ice cream	8 to 10 maraschino cherries, halved

1. Divide the fruit cocktail into four champagne glasses.
2. Divide the maraschino liqueur over.
3. Place the ice cream over the fruit cocktail and liqueur.
4. Pipe a border of whipped cream between the ice cream and the edge of the glass.
5. Drape Spun Sugar Yarn over the ice cream and glass, letting it reach to the bottom of the glass.
6. Decorate with cherry halves.

IL SORRENTO

SPUN SUGAR YARN

4 cups sugar	1 teaspoon glucose
Pinch of cream of tartar	Food coloring (optional)

1. Combine the sugar and 2 cups water in a saucepan. Heat, stirring, only until the sugar dissolves.
2. Cook to the soft-crack stage—280° on a candy thermometer.
3. Add the cream of tartar and glucose. Continue cooking to the hard-crack stage—310°. Quickly take the pan off heat and rest in a larger pan of cold water. A scant drop or two of coloring may be added at this point.
4. Move the saucepan to a warm-water bath—a larger pan or sink will do.
5. Oil either the blade of a large knife or a rolling pin. This will be the shaping base for the yarn. With a warmed spoon, scoop up some syrup and, passing the tilted spoon back and forth over the rolling pin or knife, let the syrup slowly pour to form long threads. Continue until you have as much yarn as you desire.
7. Trim the ends of the yarn. Mold, drape, or shape to suit.

Glucose can be purchased at drug stores and specialty gourmet shops.

Three Vikings

Dinner for Six

Finnish Shrimp Chowder

Marinated Cucumber Salad

Veal Norway

Danish Apple Cake

Wine:

Silver Oak Cabernet Sauvignon
or
Pinot Chardonnay

Anders Edman & Family, Owners

Anders Edman, Chef

*T*he Three Vikings restaurant is unique in the Dallas area in specializing in Swedish cuisine. In addition to other Continental fare, the menu features a variety of herring, salmon, and potato dishes, of which potato pancakes served with applesauce are a popular favorite.

Chef Anders Edman owns and operates the restaurant with other members of his family. He studied at the Culinary Institute in their native Stockholm for three years, and then worked in Europe for one year before joining the merchant marine. That employment enabled him to sail around the world eight times, which gave him a taste of virtually all the world's cuisines. He puts that knowledge to wise use in the kitchen of the Three Vikings.

It may have been a daring idea to open a restaurant which offers such an unusual cuisine, but it is one that Dallasites eagerly welcomed.

2831 Greenville Avenue

FINNISH SHRIMP CHOWDER

1 cup diced onion	2 cups clam juice
1 cup diced carrots	1 teaspoon fresh dill
1 cup diced celery	½ teaspoon ground thyme
1 cup sliced mushrooms	½ teaspoon dry mustard
¼ pound butter, melted	2 cups milk
3 tablespoons all-purpose flour	½ to 1 pound peeled baby shrimp
1 cup diced potatoes	Salt and pepper to taste
1 cup whipping cream	Dash of Worcestershire sauce
2 cups white wine	Dash of Tabasco sauce

1. Sauté the mushrooms, onions, and garlic in the butter in a large saucepan.
2. Add the flour, stirring to make a smooth paste. Cook and stir over medium heat 2 to 3 minutes.
3. Add the potatoes, cream, wine, and clam juice, stirring constantly to prevent the vegetables from sticking to the bottom of the pan.
4. Stir in the dill, thyme, mustard, and milk. Cook, stirring constantly, for 5 minutes.
5. Add the shrimp; simmer 2 to 3 minutes.
6. Add salt, pepper, and Worcestershire and Tabasco sauces to taste. Serve at once.

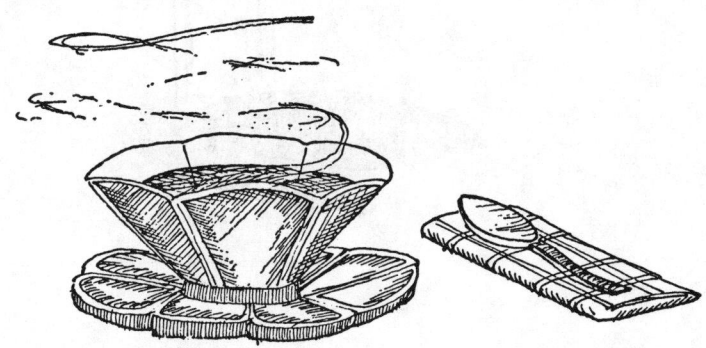

MARINATED CUCUMBER SALAD

1 tablespoon sugar
2 tablespoons finely chopped
   fresh parsley
3 large cucumbers, peeled
   and very thinly sliced

½ cup white vinegar
1 small Bermuda onion,
   chopped

Sprinkle the sugar and parsley over the cucumbers. Combine the vinegar with ½ cup water. Pour over the cucumbers and stir gently 2 to 5 minutes. Chill at least 1 hour and garnish with onion just before serving.

This salad will stay nice and crisp for two to three days if stored in a tightly closed container in the refrigerator.

VEAL NORWAY

6 (6-ounce) slices boneless
   veal
   STUFFING (see next page)
   All-purpose flour

1 egg
1 cup milk
   Bread crumbs
   Melted butter

1. Lay the veal slices between pieces of waxed paper or plastic wrap. Pound gently with a meat mallet or roll with a rolling pin until the slices are flattened, taking care not to break the meat.
2. Divide the stuffing evenly into six portions; spoon onto the center of each veal slice. Fold the slices so that the stuffing is completely sealed in; the veal will seal itself.
3. Dredge each piece in flour, then dip in a wash of the egg and milk, and dip in bread crumbs. Handle the veal carefully to keep its shape intact.
4. Sauté in melted butter over low heat for 5 minutes or more on each side, until nicely browned. Serve at once.

If a vegetable side dish is desired, fresh steamed asparagus makes a nice accompaniment.

STUFFING

½ pound mushrooms,
    coarsely chopped
2 green onions, chopped
½ clove garlic, pressed
¼ pound butter, melted
3 tablespoons all-purpose
    flour
1 cup sherry
1 cup whipping cream

½ teaspoon thyme
½ teaspoon dry mustard
1 bay leaf
½ pound shrimp, peeled
    deveined, and diced
½ pound crabmeat, in chunks
    Salt and freshly cracked
    white pepper

1. Sauté the mushrooms, onions, and garlic in the butter in a large saucepan.
2. Add the flour and blend well.
3. Add the sherry and cream, whisking constantly. Stir in the thyme and dry mustard.
4. Add the bay leaf and simmer 15 minutes.
5. Add the shrimp, crabmeat, and salt and pepper to taste; simmer 2 to 3 minutes. Cool before using.

DANISH APPLE CAKE

6 *cups sliced cooking apples*
1½ *cups plus 1 tablespoon*
  sugar
½ *teaspoon ground cinnamon*
1½ *teaspoons vanilla extract*
½ *pound butter*

3 *cups sifted fine, dry*
  bread crumbs
3 *ounces apple brandy*
½ *cup raspberry or straw-*
  berry jam or preserves
1 *cup whipping cream*

1. Combine the apples, 1 cup sugar, cinnamon, and 1 teaspoon vanilla with 1 cup hot water in a saucepan. Cook covered for 10 minutes. Drain and cool.
2. Melt the butter in a skillet over medium heat. Stir in the bread crumbs. Add ½ cup sugar and the apple brandy; stir well.
3. Spread 2 cups bread crumb mixture in a 7-inch springform pan. Spread one-half the apples over the bread crumbs, then top with one-half the jam. Repeat the layers, using 1 cup breadcrumbs and the remaining apples and jam. Top with the remaining bread crumbs. Chill at least 3 hours.
4. One hour before serving, whip the cream until stiff with the remaining 1 tablespoon sugar and ½ teaspoon vanilla. Spread over the cake. Re-chill until ready to serve.

This is even better made a day in advance because the cake is firmer on the second day.

Dinner for Four

Mussels alla Marinara

House Salad

Veal Zia Teresa

Polpette di Legumi

Strawberries Monte Bianco

Wine:

Verdicchio, Fazi Battaglia

Alberto Lombardi, Owner

Raphael Scudieri, Chef

LA TRATTORIA LOMBARDI

*J*ust slightly off the beaten track of McKinney Avenue, La Trattoria Lombardi's white building looks ever inviting. By day, it is sunny, airy, and verdant. By night, its blazing lights create an air of casual elegance. And at any time of day or night, the guests inside enjoy a special and memorable dining experience.

By featuring Northern Italian dishes with their lighter, more delicate sauces and seasonings—as well as making available a number of Southern Italian specialties—Chef Raphael Scudieri affords diners a wide selection of true Italian dishes. The pasta, soups, veal selections, and desserts are especially inspired. This is a menu that is never static; it changes every few months to take advantage of new and seasonal dishes. La Trattoria Lombardi is a restaurant for those who desire authentic and superbly prepared Italian cuisine in a warm and friendly setting.

2916 North Hall

MUSSELS ALLA MARINARA

3 *pounds mussels*
½ *bunch celery, chopped*
4 *carrots, chopped*
½ *onion, chopped*
4 *cloves garlic, chopped*

½ *teaspoon ground red*
   pepper
1 *bottle chablis*
   MARINARA SAUCE

1. Scrub the mussels with a stiff brush. Submerge in salted water for 6 hours to remove sand.
2. Place all the chopped vegetables and red pepper in a large pot; add the mussels and wine and steam 15 minutes. Strain before serving.
3. Serve the mussels in large soup bowls with Marinara Sauce poured over all.

MARINARA SAUCE

4 *cloves garlic, minced*
3 *tablespoons butter*
½ *onion, chopped*
4 *carrots, chopped*
½ *bunch celery, chopped*
2 *(28-ounce) cans peeled*
   tomatoes, drained and
   chopped

2 *teaspoons salt*
   Pepper to taste
1 *teaspoon oregano*

Brown the garlic in butter. Add the remaining ingredients and simmer 30 minutes.

HOUSE SALAD

1 small head romaine lettuce
½ green pepper, chopped
6 green olives, chopped

6 black olives, chopped
DRESSING

Wash the lettuce and tear into strips. Sprinkle with green pepper and olives. Top with dressing.

DRESSING

½ cup olive oil
2 tablespoons wine vinegar
2 anchovies, chopped
2 cloves garlic, minced

1 teaspoon oregano
1 teaspoon French mustard
½ teaspoon salt
Pepper to taste

Blend all ingredients well.

VEAL ZIA TERESA

4 (6-ounce) veal scallops
4 thin slices mozzarella
   cheese
4 thin slices prosciutto ham
½ cup flour

½ cup bread crumbs
6 tablespoons butter
½ pound mushrooms, sliced
¼ cup Madeira

1. Cut each scallop in half to make eight thin scallops. Pound each slice to flatten.
2. Place one slice of mozzarella and one slice prosciutto on each of four scallops; cover with the remaining scallops and pound the edges to seal.
3. Coat both sides of the veal "sandwiches" with flour, then with bread crumbs. Sauté in 4 tablespoons butter about 8 minutes on each side. Set aside.
4. In the same pan, sauté the mushrooms for 10 minutes in the remaining butter over low heat.
5. Add the Madeira and simmer until slightly reduced. Return the scallops to the pan and simmer 3 minutes more. Serve with sauce and mushrooms spooned over each scallop.

If you wish to make this sauce a little creamier, make a roux of flour and butter and stir it into the pan just after adding the Madeira.

POLPETTE DI LEGUMI

1 *pound spinach*
1 *eggplant, peeled and cut in large chunks*
2 *zucchini, cut in chunks*
½ *pound Parmesan cheese, grated*

3 *eggs, beaten*
3 *cloves garlic, minced*
2 *cups bread crumbs*
Salt and pepper to taste
Corn oil
TOMATO SAUCE

1. Wash and trim the spinach.
2. Boil the eggplant 30 minutes and drain. Boil the zucchini 15 minutes and drain. Boil the spinach 5 minutes and drain.
3. Grind the vegetables in a food processor or put them through a vegetable mill.
4. Reserve ¼ cup of the grated Parmesan. Add the remaining cheese, the eggs, garlic, bread crumbs, and salt and pepper to the ground vegetables. Form into patties 1 inch thick and fry in a little corn oil, turning to brown well on both sides.
5. Serve with Tomato Sauce over the top and sprinkled with reserved Parmesan.

TOMATO SAUCE

2 *(28-ounce) cans peeled tomatoes, drained and chopped*
2 *tablespoons butter*
1 *tablespoon olive oil*
1 *stalk celery, chopped*

1 *small onion, chopped*
2 *cloves garlic, chopped*
1 *tablespoon sugar*
Salt and pepper to taste
1 *teaspoon dried basil*
2 *tablespoons parsley*

1. Place the tomatoes in a sauté pan with the butter, oil, celery, onion, garlic, sugar, ½ cup water, and the salt and pepper. Bring to a boil, stirring.
2. Lower heat and simmer uncovered for 15 minutes.
3. Add the basil and parsley; continue to simmer 20 to 30 minutes, until sauce is thick.

STRAWBERRIES MONTE BIANCO

1 *quart fresh strawberries*	1 *ounce grenadine syrup*
5 *lemons*	1 *quart lemon ice*

1. Wash and hull the strawberries.
2. Squeeze the lemons and combine the juice with the grenadine.
3. Marinate the strawberries in the mixture for 1 to 2 hours.
4. Put the drained strawberries in four dessert glasses. Top each with a scoop of lemon ice and pour the marinade over all.

Lemon ice is like sherbet but without cream. Sherbet may be substituted. However, lemon ice can be purchased at Al's Imported Foods in Dallas, and other gourmet groceries elsewhere.

Appetizers

Beverages

Breads, Pasta, and Stuffing

Desserts and Dessert Accents

RECIPE INDEX

Entrées

Salads

Salad Dressings

Sauces, Stocks, and Special Seasonings

THE GREAT CHEFS SERIES
A Collection of Gourmet Recipes from the Finest Chefs in the Country

Each book contains gourmet recipes for complete meals from the chefs of 21 great restaurants.

___ *Dining In–Baltimore*	$7.95	___ *Dining In–Philadelphia* $8.95
___ *Dining In–Boston*	7.95	___ *Dining In–Phoenix* 8.95
___ *Dining In–Chicago, Vol. II*	8.95	___ *Dining In–Pittsburgh* 7.95
___ *Dining In–Cleveland*	8.95	___ *Dining In–Portland* 7.95
___ *Dining In–Dallas, Revised*	8.95	___ *Dining In–St. Louis* 7.95
___ *Dining In–Denver*	7.95	___ *Dining In–San Francisco* 7.95
___ *Dining In–Hawaii*	7.95	___ *Dining In–Seattle, Vol. II* 7.95
___ *Dining In–Houston, Vol. I*	7.95	___ *Dining In–Seattle, Vol. III* 8.95
___ *Dining In–Houston, Vol. II*	7.95	___ *Dining In–Sun Valley* 7.95
___ *Dining In–Kansas City*	7.95	___ *Dining In–Toronto* 7.95
___ *Dining In–Los Angeles*	7.95	___ *Dining In–Vancouver, B.C.* 8.95
___ *Dining In–Manhattan*	8.95	___ *Dining In–Washington, D.C.* 8.95
___ *Dining In–Milwaukee*	7.95	___ *Feasting In Atlanta* 7.95
___ *Dining In–Minneapolis/St. Paul, Vol. II* 8.95		___ *Feasting In New Orleans* 7.95
___ *Dining In–Monterey Peninsula*	7.95	_____

☐ CHECK HERE IF YOU WOULD LIKE TO HAVE A
DIFFERENT DINING IN–COOKBOOK SENT TO YOU
ONCE A MONTH

Payable by MasterCard, Visa, or C.O.D. Returnable if not satisfied.
List price plus $1.00 postage and handling for each book.

BILL TO: **SHIP TO:**

Name _____   Name _____

Address _____   Address _____

City _____ State ___ Zip _____   City _____ State ___ Zip _____

☐ Payment enclosed   ☐ Send C.O.D.   ☐ Charge

Visa # _____ Exp. Date _____

MasterCard # _____ Exp. Date _____

Signature _____

PEANUT BUTTER PUBLISHING
2445 76th Avenue S.E. • Mercer Island, WA 98040
(206) 236-1982

DAR 982